Latest Work at Home Jobs list

12/26/2019

Job Vacancies @ your finger tips

Rajesh Kunnatheeri

Copyright © 2019 Rajesh Kunnatheeri

All rights reserved.

ISBN: 9781651641651

CONTENTS

INTRODUCTION — 3
USEFUL RESOURCES — 6
TRENDING ONLINE JOBS — 7
CRAIGSLIST - WORK FROM HOME JOBS LIST — 49
REMOTEES - JOBS LIST — 140
REMOTE OK - JOBS LIST — 145
WE WORK REMOTELY — 146
CONTACT ME — 147

Introduction

Hi Friends,

I have listed below some of the work at home jobs posted in the past 48 hours. In this book (as well in all my other work from home related books) you will find hundreds of job vacancies that gets posted only 24 to 48 hours before the publishing date. This will, first give you an idea of what kind of jobs are available in the market place.

Secondly, you can immediately start applying, these jobs are too fresh, that you will not get any competitors. Probably, you could be the first to apply.

Third, there is possibility that you get some good contacts, which might turn your life into your desired path.

and fourth, you get immense of ideas by viewing these job posts, which will trigger your mind, because each book directly shows you the vacancies list. Perhaps you might have some ideas of starting your own internet business, and one of the ideas from this list, might really take you off to your destination. This book has all those elements.

This book is classified in to several sections. The first section will always be "Useful Resources". In this section, you will find few good links about the news and development that occurs in the Online Jobs domain. The next and the following sections, will be TOP vital blog links and list of jobs, that are posted only 24 to 48 hours before the publishing date.

So, let's explore the jobs. Go through all the titles, we may never know when we miss the treasure!!!

[When I say work at home jobs, I also want to mention that there could be few jobs that are not work from home in the below list. That is because, the job posters while posting the job ad, they wrongly select the "Work from home" category. So, please be advised that there is possibility of non-work from home jobs listed below, but I can assure you that majorly it is going to be home based opportunities.]

Good luck!!!

Latest Work at Home Jobs list

Useful Resources

Title	Links
✓ 7 Opportunities to Prepare for a Work at Home Career	https://ift.tt/2mzSOQ0
✓ Loss Prevention Officer - Sheraton Kansas City Hotel at Crown Center	https://ift.tt/2QcmZYN
✓ Undated Custom Editable Free Printable Calendars	https://ift.tt/2sRgN0l
✓ What Can Make The Freelancer's Lifestyle Simpler?	https://ift.tt/2PLMsJG
✓ 8 Best Residual Income Ideas to Help You Escape the Rat Race	https://ift.tt/397uk4o
✓ How to Join Pinecone Research & Why You Should	https://ift.tt/391w6Es
✓ Work at Home Transcriptionist Jobs with AlphaSights	https://ift.tt/2LKgsCq

Trending Online Jobs

In this section, you will find latest trending blog links related to online and work at home jobs. These links will certainly influence you and motivates you to reach your destination. Whether you are a newbie or a seasoned work at home professional, the information shared in this page would give you new insights towards your career growth. You will find valid links of the blog posts, beneath the pictures....

Latest Work at Home Jobs list

Latest Work at Home Jobs list

Latest Work at Home Jobs list

Latest Work at Home Jobs list

Latest Work at Home Jobs list

Latest Work at Home Jobs list

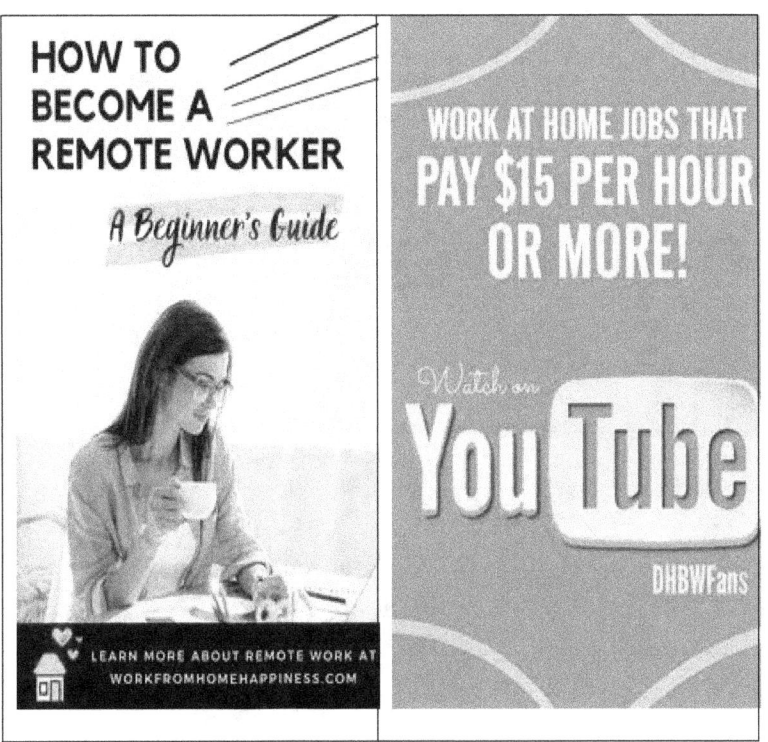

Latest Work at Home Jobs list

Latest Work at Home Jobs list

Latest Work at Home Jobs list

Latest Work at Home Jobs list

Latest Work at Home Jobs list

Latest Work at Home Jobs list

Latest Work at Home Jobs list

Latest Work at Home Jobs list

Latest Work at Home Jobs list

Latest Work at Home Jobs list

Latest Work at Home Jobs list

Latest Work at Home Jobs list

Latest Work at Home Jobs list

Latest Work at Home Jobs list

Latest Work at Home Jobs list

Latest Work at Home Jobs list

Latest Work at Home Jobs list

Latest Work at Home Jobs list

Latest Work at Home Jobs list

Latest Work at Home Jobs list

Latest Work at Home Jobs list

How to grow your social media organically in 2020 and beyond. In this article, I go over current social media trends, what you need to know to succeed, and an action plan you can follow. Grow your social organically, and for free! - https://nicolestone.com/home/how-to-grow-your-social-media-for-free

Work remotely, yet closely, with a team of receptionists operating around the country to answer calls and web chats on behalf of businesses. A fun and productive work environment that is challenging, varied, and highly rewarding. -

https://www.moneymakingmommy.com/job/work-at-home-10/

Reaching the other side of failure, overcoming adversity, is the harder part of owning a business. In our blog series, Overdraft, we asked successful business owners about their most spectacular defeats and how they survived them. Some took on massive debt. Some sold all of their belongings. And others risked everything in the pursuit of something better. Tap to read a quick round-up of 5 of our top stories from this year. -

Latest Work at Home Jobs list

https://www.shopify.com/blog/overcoming-adversity-stories

Do you love to knit, sew, make jewelry, or paint paintings? If you're artsy and crafty -- you can make good money selling your creative wares from home. Here's everything you need to know! " - https://www.theworkathomewoman.com/work-at-home-idea-arts-crafts/

Kinetix is seeking a work at home medical coder in the U.S. The company is specifically seeking an inpatient coder for this home-based

Latest Work at Home Jobs list

position. " - https://workathomemomrevolution.com/medical-billing-and-coding/kinetix-work-at-home-medical-coder-job/

We didn't start out blogging about blogging. Our fitness blog earned six figures in the first year, and we're excited to tell you how we did it. " - https://createandgo.com/make-money-with-a-fitness-blog/

Explore 10 work from home jobs legitimate money. Little to no experience required! - https://www.startamomblog.com/best-online-jobs-for-moms/

40 online business ideas that will make you a billionaire quickly. Visit this post and learn how to make money online using full-time business ideas run by millionaires in real life traditional

business environment. " -

https://www.sproutmentor.com/online-jobs/

This Hashbrown Casserole is SO simple to make in the crockpot in a pinch! -

https://moneysavingmom.com/when-you-want-to-make-hashbrown-casserole-but-you-dont-have-sour-cream/

I worked for more than a decade as a general transcriptionist - even published a book on the subject. Here's how to pass your transcription employment test. " -

https://workathomemomrevolution.com/work-at-home-transcription/how-to-pass-your-general-transcription-employment-test/

Sell Your Photos Online| Make Money Online Fast and Free. Here are 21 best places to sell your photos online and make money. Learn how to earn money from photography. " -

https://hearmefolks.com/sell-your-photos-online

Teach English online from your home. Some of these companies pay $18+ hourly! " -

https://realwaystoearnmoneyonline.com/teach-english-online/

Finding working from home too distracting? Struggling to set boundaries? Check out these five awesome tips for supercharging your productivity!   " -

https://proofreadanywhere.com/supercharge-your-productivity-as-a-

Latest Work at Home Jobs list

freelancer/

Join online Skillshare classes in art, illustration, photography, website tutorials, calligraphy, watercolor and more! - https://onefinewallet.com/free-online-courses-start-new-career/

Want to enjoy the remote life? Have no idea where or how to find work from home jobs? I'm here to help! My name is Ashlee Anderson. I'm a certified professional career coach and Forbes Coaches Council member. I specialize in remote work. Join me for a free Q&A session and ask any career questions you can think of.

Latest Work at Home Jobs list

- https://workfromhomehappiness.lpages.co/webinar-sign-up/

Looking to up your productivity? Try these twenty mom hacks to save both time and money and get a whole lot more done each day. - https://singlemomsincome.com/19-ways-to-save-time-and-money-so-you-can-be-more-productive/

Are you wondering what to sell online for easy money? Here are seven good ideas. " - https://realwaystoearnmoneyonline.com/things-you-can-sell-for-easy-money/

In my first year of recording podcast episodes, I

learned a lot of things! From how to start a podcast to how to use it for marketing, I'm here to share all of my tips with you! " - https://lindsaymaloney.com/podcast-listen/what-i-learned-in-a-year-of-podcasting/

Learn how to make money blogging with mom fitness blogs! - https://www.startamomblog.com/make-money-mom-fitness-blog/

Goggle is a popular search engine we use on a daily basis. Do you want to make money online with Google? Here are 10 Google Online Jobs you should explore even if you want to work from home or make money online. -

Latest Work at Home Jobs list

https://www.sproutmentor.com/google-jobs-online/

Wanna earn an income writing? You can by writing for blogs. Yep, you can actually ""blog"" without being a blogger. Many of these sites need writers and will pay for writers to work for them. The other perk - these are work at home jobs. Actually, many of them -- you can work anywhere that you have an internet connection. Get the details and check out this list! " -

https://www.moneymakingmommy.com/work-home-directory/blogging-jobs/

Latest Work at Home Jobs list

If you are a fast and accurate typist and love helping people, you can get paid to chat live online. The Chat Shop is hiring " -

https://www.dreamhomebasedwork.com/chat-shop-agents/

20 different ways you can work from home for Disney " - https://www.telecommutingmommies.com/how-to-work-for-disney-from-home

Want to create pinterest images that stand out and get clicks? It starts with designing clickable pinterest graphics! Follow these 27+ tips to learn exactly how to design pinterest pins to grab attention and grow your traffic. Plus, download a free pin design guide. " -

Latest Work at Home Jobs list

https://shemeansblogging.com/create-pinterest-images/

You can become a highly paid woman working from home in a relatively short period of time if you focus your energy on creating a list of subscribers first. Want to Know How To Make $200,000 Using Your Subscriber List? read my tips on how to do it! Re-pin and download my free course for entrepreneurs that want to lead a sales call that will close the deal! " -

https://www.heartcorebusiness.com/how-to-make-200000-per-year/

Latest Work at Home Jobs list

Ready to quit your day jobs? Grab this post which talks about how to start working from home today with work from home jobs that can replace your full time income. It is a great way to make money online from home for stay at home moms " - https://mrsdaakustudio.com/how-to-start-working-from-home/

Want to save MORE at restaurants? Read these dining out tips! " - https://moneysavingmom.com/how-to-save-at-restaurants/

These 7 work from home jobs are SO GOOD! I'm so happy I've found this! I've been wanting to work from home for a LONG TIME and now I have some AWESOME options! Definitely pinning for later! - https://www.chasingfoxes.com/7-work-from-home-jobs/

Want to make money from home as a data entry clerk? Here are 10 best data entry jobs from home to get you started! You get to work from home whenever you want and earn however much money you want especially with Fiverr! " - https://earnsmartonlineclass.com/data-entry-jobs-from-home/

Latest Work at Home Jobs list

Craigslist - Work from home Jobs list

Caution : Craigslist is one of the largest job boards out there in US. It generally skews toward lower skilled or temporary positions but is a fantastic resource for most jobs. Each day there are thousands of work from home jobs getting posted in Craigslist and I did my level best to remove jobs that are not a Work from Home. For Eg., I searched for the following phrases in the report, - driver, CDL, dog, plumber, carpenter, caregiver, handyman, cleaner, cleaning, surrogate, cook, electrician, installers, owner operators, road, roofers, painters, dishwasher, house keeper etc., - and removed those jobs from the list to make it more related to work from home. However, it is highly impossible for me to check each job and see if it is spam or real job vacancy. Just because there is good amount of spam jobs, we should not let genuine and good work from home opportunity to slip through our fingers.

Title	Links
1. Travel Agents Wanted Working From Home!!! ((((Nationwide))))	https://ift.tt/2Qhb8lW
2. Graphic Designer + Produce and Maintain Social Media, Website,	https://ift.tt/2ZicRlt

Latest Work at Home Jobs list

Digital (Orange County)	
3. * * * Want to Be a Millionaire? * * * Get FREE Millionaire Training! (Dallas DFW and surrounding areas)	https://ift.tt/2MmYqan
4. State Farm Insurance Agency (pittsburg / antioch)	https://ift.tt/2MlzXSW
5. Territory Sales Manager - South Florida (Sunrise, FL)	https://ift.tt/2ZfDyax
6. Looking for part time tutor (cambridge)	https://ift.tt/394KyeP
7. Be Your Own Boss-Work From Home PT/FT $750-$5000 Per Week (Atlanta)	https://ift.tt/2tKfT6l
8. Experienced Personal Assistant (Venice)	https://ift.tt/34PKPz1
9. Dairy Queen (Appomattox)	https://ift.tt/373jY3Y
10. Day Trade Our Money as a FOREX Currency Trader - Up to $100,000! (On Line at Home or Office)	https://ift.tt/2PQypTe

Latest Work at Home Jobs list

11. ***Earn Over $50K - Unique Marketing Opportunity	https://ift.tt/2ZgzZke
12. Part Time Administrative Assistant- Work from Home (Victor)	https://ift.tt/34P88J1
13. Work Smarter Not Harder NO Touch/ Drop and Hook Home Weekends	https://ift.tt/2tGb51D
14. Outbound Sales Reps! Unlimited earning ~ Large daily $ spiff! (Springfield)	https://ift.tt/2MoQ8Pg
15. Business secretary, London (London, Canary Wharf)	https://ift.tt/34MTPF2
16. Join the Number One Real Estate Team in MN- Show/List Homes This Week! (entire Twin Cities area)	https://ift.tt/37dkrkf
17. Get paid to shop! Have a car? Earn $$$ delivering for Instacart	https://ift.tt/2ZeQYUa
18. LVN -FT Senior Living Community (119) (Cerritos)	https://ift.tt/2QbqJd7
19. Part Time Openings - Paid Weekly - Interview Right Away (Blue Bell, Plymouth Meeting, Ambler)	https://ift.tt/2MoJLM5

Latest Work at Home Jobs list

20. Part Time Openings - Paid Weekly - Interview Right Away (Tolland, Manchester, Gales Ferry)	https://ift.tt/2Zjp8pV
21. Entry-level Customer Sales, Apply Immediately (Norcross, Johns Creek, Lake Lanier)	https://ift.tt/373Vs2E
22. Part Time Openings - Paid Weekly - Interview Right Away (Andover, Tewksbury, Haverhill)	https://ift.tt/2rq4RlW
23. Immediate part time sales: flexible schedules (Miami, Doral, Coral Gables)	https://ift.tt/2QeqzBz
24. Part Time Openings - Paid Weekly - Interview Right Away (Hanover, Catasauqua)	https://ift.tt/2PTgRWF
25. Part Time Openings - Paid Weekly - Interview Right Away (Natick, Wellesley, Framingham)	https://ift.tt/2MmiJoA
26. Part Time Openings - Paid Weekly - Interview Right Away (Garden City, Cranston, Providence)	https://ift.tt/2QgeJXB

Latest Work at Home Jobs list

27. Part Time Openings - Paid Weekly - Interview Right Away (Orlando, Winter Park)	https://ift.tt/2EMBNbl
28. Part Time Openings - Paid Weekly - Interview Right Away (Raleigh, Cary, Apex)	https://ift.tt/2rmonzL
29. Part Time Openings - Paid Weekly - Interview Right Away (Cherry Hill, Voorhees)	https://ift.tt/2Zfuy5d
30. Part Time Openings - Paid Weekly - Interview Right Away (Charleston)	https://ift.tt/2PQSqJ7
31. Part Time Openings - Paid Weekly - Interview Right Away (Paramus, Fort Lee, Hasbrouck Heights)	https://ift.tt/2EOFyNv
32. Part Time Openings - Paid Weekly - Interview Right Away (Hamden, Branford)	https://ift.tt/376OwBV
33. Part Time Openings - Paid Weekly - Interview Right Away (Marshalls Creek, Hazleton)	https://ift.tt/2MoNKYT
34. Part Time Openings - Paid Weekly -	https://ift.tt/2SkLtC

Latest Work at Home Jobs list

	Interview Right Away (Virginia Beach, Newport News, Chesapeake)	0
35.	Part Time Openings - Paid Weekly - Interview Right Away (Levittown, Commack, Bohemia)	https://ift.tt/2QbqUVW
36.	Part Time Openings - Paid Weekly - Interview Right Away (Charlotte, Matthews, Mint Hill)	https://ift.tt/2ZjsdGm
37.	Part Time Openings - Paid Weekly - Interview Right Away (Towson, Bel Air, Finksburg)	https://ift.tt/373xzIk
38.	Part Time Openings - Paid Weekly - Interview Right Away (Pittsford, Penfield, Fairport)	https://ift.tt/2EMQiMs
39.	Part Time Openings - Paid Weekly - Interview Right Away (Tallahassee, Wakulla)	https://ift.tt/2Mlh7v2
40.	Entry-level Customer Sales, Apply Immediately (Fairfield, Greenwich, Milford)	https://ift.tt/2SmQ1HJ
41.	Part Time Openings - Paid Weekly -	https://ift.tt/2sRGf

Latest Work at Home Jobs list

Interview Right Away (Jacksonville, Ponte Vedra)	CV
42. LPN-Licensed Practical Nurse-Senior Living Community (245) (Naples)	https://ift.tt/2sUAmoE
43. Entry-level Customer Sales, Apply Immediately (North Ft Myers, Ft Myers Beach, Sanibel)	https://ift.tt/34TbmeC
44. Part Time Openings - Paid Weekly - Interview Right Away (Columbia, Lexington, Irmo)	https://ift.tt/2SiB61h
45. Part Time Openings - Paid Weekly - Interview Right Away (Rockville)	https://ift.tt/2rq8Y1m
46. Immediate part time sales: flexible schedules (Bedford, Lexington)	https://ift.tt/2EIPI7E
47. Part Time Openings - Paid Weekly - Interview Right Away (Howell, Jackson, Brick)	https://ift.tt/2PRea7V
48. Business Loan Advisor - Salary/Commission/Bonus (Remote) (Orange County (Remote))	https://ift.tt/2SILSUK

Latest Work at Home Jobs list

49. Part Time Openings - Paid Weekly - Interview Right Away (Farmington, Bloomfield, Canton)	https://ift.tt/34RtOUZ
50. Part Time Openings - Paid Weekly - Interview Right Away (Frederick, Hagerstown, Urbana)	https://ift.tt/35UI3K0
51. Part Time Openings - Paid Weekly - Interview Right Away (Grandview, Columbus, Upper Arlington)	https://ift.tt/2MmoORW
52. Part Time Openings - Paid Weekly - Interview Right Away (Newburgh, Fishkill, Middletown)	https://ift.tt/3990Ov6
53. Part Time Openings - Paid Weekly - Interview Right Away (Castleton, Carmel, Fishers)	https://ift.tt/34VTboQ
54. Get paid to shop! Join Instacart's growing in-store team!	https://ift.tt/2PNvASG
55. Now Hiring Media Sales Rep, Work from home (Kansas City, MO)	https://ift.tt/2MlmaM6
56. CHHA (Bergen County)	https://ift.tt/34OGBrj

Latest Work at Home Jobs list

57. Part Time Openings - Paid Weekly - Interview Right Away (Tampa, Carrollwood)	https://ift.tt/2SqXBBv
58. Director of Youth Ministry (Harrison)	https://ift.tt/35SEwvH
59. Part Time Openings - Paid Weekly - Interview Right Away (Blue Ash, Anderson, Kenwood)	https://ift.tt/2rqc31s
60. Med Aide - Assisted Living- Senior Living Community (226) (Sherman Oaks)	https://ift.tt/2PNRJAr
61. Medication Aide PT Memory Care - Senior Living Community (226) (Sherman Oaks)	https://ift.tt/395HKy2
62. Part Time Openings - Paid Weekly - Interview Right Away (Cheektowaga, Amherst, Buffalo)	https://ift.tt/34VUp3q
63. Part Time Openings - Paid Weekly - Interview Right Away (The Valley, Liberty Lake)	https://ift.tt/395LAXY
64. Part Time Openings - Paid Weekly -	https://ift.tt/2Qgm2

Latest Work at Home Jobs list

Interview Right Away (Sandy, American Fork, Herriman)	P1
65. Part Time Openings - Paid Weekly - Interview Right Away (Fairlawn, Atwater, Canton)	https://ift.tt/35PatoE
66. Part Time Openings - Paid Weekly - Interview Right Away (Fairfax, Gainesville, Warrenton)	https://ift.tt/2tDYD2q
67. Music Teachers Needed -- All Instruments! (NoVA, D.C., and MD)	https://ift.tt/2siaSS7
68. Part Time Openings - Paid Weekly - Interview Right Away (Nashville, Bellevue, Brentwood)	https://ift.tt/2QbYFq2
69. Part Time Openings - Paid Weekly - Interview Right Away (Ocala, Bellview, Lecanto)	https://ift.tt/34L7dcE
70. Entry-level Customer Sales, Apply Immediately (Lakeland, Eaton Park)	https://ift.tt/2Mo6Dez
71. Part Time Openings - Paid Weekly - Interview Right Away (Edina, Chanhassen, Minneapolis)	https://ift.tt/2ELmWht

Latest Work at Home Jobs list

72. Part Time Openings - Paid Weekly - Interview Right Away (Franklin Park, Bowling Green, Holland)	https://ift.tt/2SfM9Zg
73. Part Time Openings - Paid Weekly - Interview Right Away (South Hills, Canonsburg, Elizabeth)	https://ift.tt/2MmZI5b
74. Part Time Openings - Paid Weekly - Interview Right Away (Morgantown, Bruceton Mills, Kingwood)	https://ift.tt/2PQBF0Y
75. Part Time Openings - Paid Weekly - Interview Right Away (Ocala, Lake City, Gainesville)	https://ift.tt/2PQHfAg
76. Part Time Openings - Paid Weekly - Interview Right Away (Appleton, De Pere, Hortonville)	https://ift.tt/2ZhSO6F
77. Part Time Openings - Paid Weekly - Interview Right Away (Omaha, Bellevue, Council Bluffs)	https://ift.tt/2QqABQv
78. Part Time Openings - Paid Weekly - Interview Right Away (Rocky River, Amherst, Berea)	https://ift.tt/2sU4AIg

Latest Work at Home Jobs list

79. Part Time Openings - Paid Weekly - Interview Right Away (East Lansing, Dewitt, Grand Ledge)	https://ift.tt/2Svo80z
80. Part Time Openings - Paid Weekly - Interview Right Away (Guilderland, Amsterdam, Clifton Park)	https://ift.tt/2Zf5v2a
81. Part Time Openings - Paid Weekly - Interview Right Away (Warren, Grosse Pointe, Harrison Township)	https://ift.tt/374qtn3
82. Part Time Openings - Paid Weekly - Interview Right Away (Boise, Caldwell, Eagle)	https://ift.tt/2PQCBm0
83. Part Time Openings - Paid Weekly - Interview Right Away (Savannah, Pooler, Hinesville)	https://ift.tt/395DHSn
84. Part Time Openings - Paid Weekly - Interview Right Away (Windsor Heights, Clive, Urbandale)	https://ift.tt/34L9mol
85. $5000-$10000+ A Month- Start Immediately! (Nationwide)	https://ift.tt/2ZhU49T
86. Part Time Openings - Paid Weekly -	https://ift.tt/2MoUY

Latest Work at Home Jobs list

Interview Right Away (Northbrook, Wilmette, Evanston)	w9
87. Part Time Openings - Paid Weekly - Interview Right Away (DeWitt, Fayetteville)	https://ift.tt/2SjLTsb
88. Part Time Openings - Paid Weekly - Interview Right Away (Fayetteville, Woodfield)	https://ift.tt/2sVC6Ot
89. Part Time Openings - Paid Weekly - Interview Right Away (Erie, Albion, Edinboro)	https://ift.tt/35RAXWG
90. Part Time Openings - Paid Weekly - Interview Right Away (Grand Rapids, Ada, Allendale)	https://ift.tt/35M9k1b
91. Part Time Openings - Paid Weekly - Interview Right Away (North Logan, Smithfield)	https://ift.tt/2tMiMDF
92. Part Time Openings - Paid Weekly - Interview Right Away (Lenexa, Overland Park)	https://ift.tt/34OLzEt
93. Part Time Openings - Paid Weekly -	https://ift.tt/2ESzZ

Latest Work at Home Jobs list

Interview Right Away (Piedmont, Powedersville, Greenwood)	0h
94. Over $15.00 Per Hour + Bonuses Canvassers Needed (Phoenix)	https://ift.tt/35Peh9q
95. Part Time Openings - Paid Weekly - Interview Right Away (Mehlville, Arnold, Columbia)	https://ift.tt/2ZiQ09f
96. Part Time Openings - Paid Weekly - Interview Right Away (York, Dover)	https://ift.tt/2MoVw5b
97. Part Time Openings - Paid Weekly - Interview Right Away (Billings, Laurel)	https://ift.tt/2Mo9Haz
98. Part Time Openings - Paid Weekly - Interview Right Away (Jeffersontown)	https://ift.tt/2sZhGEk
99. Part Time Openings - Paid Weekly - Interview Right Away (Lexington, Berea, Harrodsburg)	https://ift.tt/35R4TSR
100. Part Time Openings - Paid Weekly - Interview Right Away (Daytona Beach, Ormond Beach)	https://ift.tt/34PaMOY
101. Part Time Openings - Paid	https://ift.tt/2PTt7q

Latest Work at Home Jobs list

Weekly - Interview Right Away (Greenville, Centerville, Xenia)	9
102. Part Time Openings - Paid Weekly - Interview Right Away (Provo, Orem)	https://ift.tt/2ELC5PB
103. Part Time Openings - Paid Weekly - Interview Right Away (Rocky Mount, Greenville, Winerville)	https://ift.tt/2PQ9b7I
104. Part Time Openings - Paid Weekly - Interview Right Away (Tequesta, Jupiter, West Palm Beach)	https://ift.tt/34OAcwb
105. Part Time Openings - Paid Weekly - Interview Right Away (Macon, Byron)	https://ift.tt/396sEII
106. Part Time Openings - Paid Weekly - Interview Right Away (Cedar Rapids, Coralville)	https://ift.tt/2rmzKaV
107. Part Time Openings - Paid Weekly - Interview Right Away (Idaho Falls, Ammon, Lincoln)	https://ift.tt/2s5cYVv

Latest Work at Home Jobs list

108.	Part Time Openings - Paid Weekly - Interview Right Away (LaGrange, Columbus, Whitewater Estates)	https://ift.tt/2QbFeO5
109.	Office Assistant (Work From Home) (All of Pennsylvania)	https://ift.tt/2tLj2CV
110.	Immediate part time sales: flexible schedules (Coon Rapids, Anoka, Champlin)	https://ift.tt/2ZjDzdB
111.	Part Time Openings - Paid Weekly - Interview Right Away (Cedar Park, Leander, Dripping Springs)	https://ift.tt/370tZic
112.	Part Time Openings - Paid Weekly - Interview Right Away (Green Bay, Bellevue, Krakow)	https://ift.tt/2POHBaG
113.	Immediate Remote Work - Customer Sales/Service - Paid Weekly (Grantsville)	https://ift.tt/34SmAzU
114.	Part Time Openings - Paid Weekly - Interview Right Away	https://ift.tt/2MkmLgX

Latest Work at Home Jobs list

(Altoona, Johnstown, Indiana)	
115. Part Time Openings - Paid Weekly - Interview Right Away (Casper, Douglas, Evansville)	https://ift.tt/2MlWhfl
116. Part Time Openings - Paid Weekly - Interview Right Away (Freeport, Forreston, DeKalb)	https://ift.tt/34Tmecq
117. Part Time Openings - Paid Weekly - Interview Right Away (Ann Arbor, Brighton, Hartland)	https://ift.tt/2tJ6yvr
118. Part Time Openings - Paid Weekly - Interview Right Away (Kalamazoo, Portage)	https://ift.tt/2SjXozO
119. Hiring Event 1/6/2020 - Direct Care /Ypsilanti	https://ift.tt/2Q9QtGK
120. Part Time Openings - Paid Weekly - Interview Right Away (Arden)	https://ift.tt/2MknEpN
121. Part Time Openings - Paid Weekly - Interview Right Away (St George, Cedar City)	https://ift.tt/34S4tdq

Latest Work at Home Jobs list

122.	Part Time Openings - Paid Weekly - Interview Right Away (Melbourne, Cocoa Beach, Titusville)	https://ift.tt/2SgCt0F
123.	Part Time Openings - Paid Weekly - Interview Right Away (Mankato, New Ulm)	https://ift.tt/35S9Drp
124.	Part Time Openings - Paid Weekly - Interview Right Away (Summerfield, Oak Ridge, Greensboro)	https://ift.tt/2POZV3q
125.	Part Time Openings - Paid Weekly - Interview Right Away (Plano, Allen, Lewisville)	https://ift.tt/2ZiTWH3
126.	Part Time Openings - Paid Weekly - Interview Right Away (Friendswood, Alvin, Katy)	https://ift.tt/2QcEAzZ
127.	$1,000 TO $2,000+/DAY TAKING INBOUND CALLS AT HOME - PROOF INSIDE! ((OUR #1 REP EARNS OVER $300,000/MONTH (FULLY	https://ift.tt/2Mmxacg

Latest Work at Home Jobs list

VERIFIABLE)	
128. Part Time Openings - Paid Weekly - Interview Right Away (Boca Raton, Delray)	https://ift.tt/2QqES6v
129. Part Time Openings - Paid Weekly - Interview Right Away (North Chesterfield, Henrico)	https://ift.tt/2ShTo2G
130. Immediate part time sales: flexible schedules (Oak Brook, Berwyn, Joliet)	https://ift.tt/2SIbm4k
131. Entry-level Customer Sales, Apply Immediately (Palatine, Barrington, Fox River Grove)	https://ift.tt/396EkLr
132. Part Time Openings - Paid Weekly - Interview Right Away (Columbia, Ashland, Booneville)	https://ift.tt/2PSLYl8
133. Part Time Openings - Paid Weekly - Interview Right Away (College Station, Brazos Valley, Brenham)	https://ift.tt/2sUMGVW
134. Immediate Remote Work -	https://ift.tt/2sXnzI

Latest Work at Home Jobs list

Customer Sales/Service - Paid Weekly (Wolf Point)	4
135. Part Time Openings - Paid Weekly - Interview Right Away (Scottsdale, Cave Creek, Fountain Hills)	https://ift.tt/2t02UwI
136. Immediate part time sales: flexible schedules (New Port Richey, Port Richey)	https://ift.tt/2t02V3K
137. Part Time Openings - Paid Weekly - Interview Right Away (Littleton, Centennial, Highlands Ranch)	https://ift.tt/2PO4hrx
138. Part Time Openings - Paid Weekly - Interview Right Away (McAllen, Edinburg, Donna)	https://ift.tt/2SiMev5
139. RN or LPN with Vent Experience for Private Duty up to $40/hr (Plymouth)	https://ift.tt/2sdHaO5
140. Part-time Operations Team Member - Miami, FL	https://ift.tt/396Zrxa

Latest Work at Home Jobs list

141. Part Time Openings - Paid Weekly - Interview Right Away (Pasadena, Glendale)	https://ift.tt/2QbbSiM
142. Immediate Remote Work - Customer Sales/Service - Paid Weekly (Augusta, Gardiner, Waterville)	https://ift.tt/2SIcepC
143. Part Time Openings - Paid Weekly - Interview Right Away (Oklahoma City, Bethany, Choctaw)	https://ift.tt/35PSQ89
144. Executive Assistant Needed (Billings, MT)	https://ift.tt/34Vyw4h
145. Part Time Openings - Paid Weekly - Interview Right Away (Las Vegas, Centennial Hills)	https://ift.tt/2PR7wON
146. Part Time Openings - Paid Weekly - Interview Right Away (Lubbock, Abernathy, Brownfield)	https://ift.tt/2EOE2Lm
147. Afterschool Substitute Teacher at JCC East Bay (berkeley)	https://ift.tt/2SiXiZi
148. Behavior Technicians at	https://ift.tt/34RDL

Latest Work at Home Jobs list

	Advanced ABA (santa clara)	BP
149.	Cable Technician -will train - co. gas card & vehicle (concord / pleasant hill / martinez)	https://ift.tt/2sV73lJ
150.	Cable Technician - will Train - co. vehicle & gas card (richmond / point / annex)	https://ift.tt/2shSGYC
151.	Cable Technician - will train! Co-Vehicle & Gas Card (hayward / castro valley)	https://ift.tt/2Zie4Jk
152.	Cable Technician - will train - co. vehicle & gas card (fairfield / vacaville)	https://ift.tt/2EJ1o4S
153.	Cable Technician - Petaluma, CA (petaluma)	https://ift.tt/34LJl8F
154.	Cable Technician (Sacramento)	https://ift.tt/2SkW3sH
155.	Part Time Openings - Paid Weekly - Interview Right Away (Elk Grove, Fair Oaks)	https://ift.tt/35UTAZO
156.	SELPA Specialist (Oroville)	https://ift.tt/2PQdte

Latest Work at Home Jobs list

	X
157. Immediate Remote Work - Customer Sales/Service - Paid Weekly (Concord, Manchester, Dover)	https://ift.tt/2tLtYR0
158. Server/ Dietary Aide	https://ift.tt/2ZgJIap
159. Server / Dietary Aide - openings throughout the Twin Cities	https://ift.tt/2PTRcNv
160. Immediate Remote Work - Customer Sales/Service - Paid Weekly (Lewiston, Clarkston)	https://ift.tt/361CJVr
161. ***Be Your Own Boss*** (Nationwide)	https://ift.tt/34T7GcK
162. Levy at Moda Center ~ HIRING Sanitation Coordinator $15-$17/hr (Portland)	https://ift.tt/2SIWvqC
163. YES Support Staff (NE Portland)	https://ift.tt/372nawz
164. Part Time Openings - Paid Weekly - Interview Right Away	https://ift.tt/2ZiDnuV

Latest Work at Home Jobs list

	(Clackamas, Gresham, Lake Oswego)	
165.	Part Time Openings - Paid Weekly - Interview Right Away (San Antonio, Bulverde, Canyon Springs)	https://ift.tt/35QETXP
166.	#1 Atlanta RE/MAX Team. AGENTS, it's all about the LEADS!!! (Atlanta)	https://ift.tt/2ZitJZ9
167.	Part Time Openings - Paid Weekly - Interview Right Away (Wasilla, Chugiak, Anchorage)	https://ift.tt/2rmFJfT
168.	Immediate Remote Work - Customer Sales/Service - Paid Weekly (Great Falls)	https://ift.tt/35XdBz6
169.	Part Time Openings - Paid Weekly - Interview Right Away (Salem, Keizer)	https://ift.tt/2MlvVtC
170.	Part Time Openings - Paid Weekly - Interview Right Away (San Marcos, Buda)	https://ift.tt/2Mn5CTQ
171.	Part Time Openings - Paid	https://ift.tt/39auyb

Latest Work at Home Jobs list

Weekly - Interview Right Away (Anaheim, Fullerton, La Habra)	k
172. Personal/executive assistant for eclectic tasks (Glenwood/State St. area)	https://ift.tt/2sSFs4O
173. Part Time Openings - Paid Weekly - Interview Right Away (Amarillo, Canyon, Dumas)	https://ift.tt/2EJcyGX
174. $10k - $20k or more monthly potential. (Nationwide)	https://ift.tt/34VBFkB
175. Part Time Openings - Paid Weekly - Interview Right Away (Seattle, Edmonds, Kent)	https://ift.tt/35OOUoo
176. Part Time Openings - Paid Weekly - Interview Right Away (Ventura, Camarillo)	https://ift.tt/35SRucR
177. Immediate Remote Work - Customer Sales/Service - Paid Weekly (Nevada)	https://ift.tt/35QZhbd
178. Part Time Openings - Paid Weekly - Interview Right Away	https://ift.tt/2Mm22cX

Latest Work at Home Jobs list

(Modesto, Ripon, Oakdale)	
179. Part Time Openings - Paid Weekly - Interview Right Away (Tucson, Marana, Nogales)	https://ift.tt/2Zka3Ec
180. Immediate Remote Work - Customer Sales/Service - Paid Weekly (Jackson)	https://ift.tt/2ZpToiU
181. Part Time Openings - Paid Weekly - Interview Right Away (Mission Valley, San Diego, Beach Cities)	https://ift.tt/2Q9VbUW
182. Part Time Openings - Paid Weekly - Interview Right Away (Bakersfield)	https://ift.tt/35PmxGs
183. Immediate Remote Work - Customer Sales/Service - Paid Weekly (Salina)	https://ift.tt/2EOhOJm
184. Immediate part time sales: flexible schedules (Anthem, Phoenix)	https://ift.tt/2se7Nm0
185. ***Bilingual Office Coordinator*** (Denville)	https://ift.tt/2PP5Ghy

Latest Work at Home Jobs list

186. Immediate Remote Work - Customer Sales/Service - Paid Weekly (Pullman, Moscow)	https://ift.tt/2sRXwMh
187. Part Time Openings - Paid Weekly - Interview Right Away (Fort Collins, Wellington, Windsor)	https://ift.tt/2SkJxcE
188. Immediate Remote Work - Customer Sales/Service - Paid Weekly (Kalispell)	https://ift.tt/36ZNhnZ
189. Mover/Helper for Local Santa Rosa Moving Company (santa rosa)	https://ift.tt/34PiyZa
190. Part Time Openings - Paid Weekly - Interview Right Away (Walnut Creek, Fremont, Fairfield)	https://ift.tt/35Rd2Xr
191. Part Time Openings - Paid Weekly - Interview Right Away (Chico, Paradise)	https://ift.tt/34LPsK9
192. Immediate Remote Work - Customer Sales/Service - Paid Weekly (Missoula)	https://ift.tt/2MmD4tW
193. Part Time Openings - Paid	https://ift.tt/374Agtj

Latest Work at Home Jobs list

Weekly - Interview Right Away (Fresno, Clovis, Kerman)	
194. Part Time Openings - Paid Weekly - Interview Right Away (Colorado Springs, Falcon, Peyton)	https://ift.tt/2PRcjjf
195. Immediate Remote Work - Customer Sales/Service - Paid Weekly (Kirksville)	https://ift.tt/2EK5ud2
196. Part Time Openings - Paid Weekly - Interview Right Away (Riverside, Grand Terrace, Victorville)	https://ift.tt/2shYBgi
197. Part Time Openings - Paid Weekly - Interview Right Away (Albuquerque, Belen)	https://ift.tt/3996ULY
198. Entry Level Sales Representative (Austin, TX)	https://ift.tt/2PRvdqr
199. Part Time Openings - Paid Weekly - Interview Right Away (Las Cruces)	https://ift.tt/2MoxDuj
200. Entry Level Sales	https://ift.tt/396Kp

Latest Work at Home Jobs list

	Representative (San Antonio, TX)	HL
201.	Part Time Openings - Paid Weekly - Interview Right Away (El Paso, Socorro, West El Paso)	https://ift.tt/34QGagf
202.	Part Time Openings - Paid Weekly - Interview Right Away (Temple, Belton, Copperas Cove)	https://ift.tt/2QcaNay
203.	Entry Level Sales Representative (Atlanta, GA)	https://ift.tt/397Orjd
204.	Entry Level Sales Representative (East TX - Tyler, Etc.)	https://ift.tt/377laTX
205.	Entry Level Sales Representative (Little Rock, AR)	https://ift.tt/34QllvR
206.	Entry Level Sales Representative	https://ift.tt/2EQqYos
207.	Shared Living Provider/Work From Home- South County (North Kingstown)	https://ift.tt/2Mkvrnx
208.	Shared Living Provider/Work From Home-East Bay (Barrington)	https://ift.tt/372t4hd

Latest Work at Home Jobs list

209.	Shared Living Provider/Work From Home- Newport County (Newport)	https://ift.tt/35PZj2V
210.	Service Coordinator (Medford)	https://ift.tt/35SWr5k
211.	Shared Living Provider/Work From Home- Kent County (Warwick)	https://ift.tt/2tLre68
212.	Entry Level Sales Representative (Memphis, TN)	https://ift.tt/35QKw8p
213.	Care Giver for Mom with Dementia needed (Keyport, NJ)	https://ift.tt/2SI4GDc
214.	Entry Level Sales Representative (Lansing, MI)	https://ift.tt/34QmdGf
215.	Sleep Coordinator (Rockwall)	https://ift.tt/2EJgS99
216.	Entry Level Sales Representative (Dallas)	https://ift.tt/2PRtuS3
217.	customer service reps for great company (houston)	https://ift.tt/2PNTNs5
218.	Entry Level Sales Representative (Fayetteville, AR)	https://ift.tt/3976xli

Latest Work at Home Jobs list

219. Life Insurance Sales (Hartford, CT)	https://ift.tt/2PPYt0v
220. Entry Level Sales Representative (Detroit, MI)	https://ift.tt/393j4WS
221. Entry Level Sales Representative (Jonesboro, AR)	https://ift.tt/2si0ARM
222. Entry Level Sales Representative (Columbia, MO)	https://ift.tt/2PRu8Pt
223. Entry Level Sales Representative (Southern MD)	https://ift.tt/2SmgSUo
224. Entry Level Sales Representative (Grand Rapids, MI)	https://ift.tt/34Lnqi0
225. Immediate part time sales: flexible schedules (Chula Vista, Bonita)	https://ift.tt/35MlQhb
226. Entry Level Sales Representative (Kansas City, MO)	https://ift.tt/396M6VD
227. Entry Level Sales Representative (College Station TX)	https://ift.tt/2sS1zYZ
228. Entry Level Sales	https://ift.tt/2ZjOkN1

Latest Work at Home Jobs list

	Representative (Charleston, SC)	
229.	Entry Level Sales Representative (St Louis, MO)	https://ift.tt/2Mpj0H8
230.	Entry Level Sales Representative (Greenville, SC)	https://ift.tt/2tNMCrz
231.	Business Loan Advisor- Position is base + bonus + commission (Remote) (Pheonix)	https://ift.tt/2EJhJqn
232.	Entry Level Sales Representative (Lawrence, KS	https://ift.tt/2SiUfjF
233.	Part Time Openings - Paid Weekly - Interview Right Away (Tulsa, Claremore, Bixby)	https://ift.tt/35SXtye
234.	Entry Level Sales Representative (Tulsa, OK)	https://ift.tt/2tLt2vX
235.	Life Insurance Sales (New Haven, CT)	https://ift.tt/2EJ81UW
236.	Entry Level Sales Representative (Springfield, MO)	https://ift.tt/2MndcOl
237.	Entry Level Sales	https://ift.tt/34MJ6u5

Latest Work at Home Jobs list

Representative (Topeka, KS)	
238. Entry Level Sales Representative (Florence, SC)	https://ift.tt/393dHa5
239. PREFER TO WORK FROM HOME? (Los Angeles)	https://ift.tt/2EL9auW
240. Part Time Openings - Paid Weekly - Interview Right Away (Burbank, Granada Hills, Porter Ranch)	https://ift.tt/2EP8F3k
241. Immediate part time work: flexible schedules (Lakewood, Cypress, Lawndale)	https://ift.tt/2SreX17
242. Immediate Remote Work - Customer Sales/Service - Paid Weekly (Phillipsburg)	https://ift.tt/2PPF2F3
243. Entry Level Sales Representative (Oklahoma City, OK)	https://ift.tt/374iUNe
244. Entry Level Sales Representative (Lexington, KY)	https://ift.tt/2ENmOoO
245. Immediate Openings - Customer Sales/Service - Apply Now	https://ift.tt/2PNOqZU

Latest Work at Home Jobs list

	(Kalamazoo, Portage)	
246.	Entry Level Sales Representative (Bowling Green, KY)	https://ift.tt/2SI6hJC
247.	Part Time Openings - Paid Weekly - Interview Right Away (Boulder, Lafayette)	https://ift.tt/2Zi8NSd
248.	Part Time Openings - Paid Weekly - Interview Right Away (Santa Fe, Las Vegas, Mora)	https://ift.tt/34OZEBP
249.	Entry Level Sales Representative (Baltimore, MD)	https://ift.tt/35QSChl
250.	Entry-level Customer Sales, Apply Immediately (Huntsville, Brownsboro, Madison)	https://ift.tt/2MnenNL
251.	Entry Level Sales Representative (Wichita, KS)	https://ift.tt/396EG4Q
252.	Part Time Openings - Paid Weekly - Interview Right Away (Laredo, Zapata)	https://ift.tt/2rnMDI5
253.	Immediate Openings - Customer Sales/Service - Apply Now	https://ift.tt/35SY7ff

Latest Work at Home Jobs list

(Conneaut Lake, Saegertown)	
254. Part Time Openings - Paid Weekly - Interview Right Away (Baton Rouge, Prairieville)	https://ift.tt/375DPPl
255. Entry Level Sales Representative (Macon, GA)	https://ift.tt/34Szzl8
256. Immediate Openings - Customer Sales/Service - Apply Now (Peoria, Bloomington, Canton)	https://ift.tt/2Qcjxxf
257. Entry Level Sales Representative (Columbia, SC)	https://ift.tt/34TyvO2
258. Part Time Openings - Paid Weekly - Interview Right Away (Waco, Stephenville, Lingleville)	https://ift.tt/2Zhe0cW
259. Immediate Remote Work - Customer Sales/Service - Paid Weekly (Bemidji)	https://ift.tt/2Sg2gGe
260. Entry Level Sales Representative (Nashville, TN)	https://ift.tt/2EJdif4
261. Life Insurance Sales	https://ift.tt/2SrgJ2h

Latest Work at Home Jobs list

262.	Senior Accountant - Part Time, Flex Hours (Nashville)	https://ift.tt/2rkV2pe
263.	Entry-level Customer Sales, Apply Immediately (Mobile, Bay Minette, Daphne)	https://ift.tt/2tGHZ29
264.	Immediate Openings - Customer Sales/Service - Apply Now (Monroe)	https://ift.tt/392QSDH
265.	Full-Time Customer Service Representative (Lakeway)	https://ift.tt/2Qhfb8f
266.	Business Loan Advisor- Position is base + bonus + commission (Remote) (Austin)	https://ift.tt/2rqw8Vo
267.	Nurse Practitioner (Multiple)	https://ift.tt/2tLuyhC
268.	Senior Accountant - Part Time, Flex Hours (Austin, TX)	https://ift.tt/2SkPgza
269.	Congregate Meal Sites Coordinator	https://ift.tt/34Mk9PD
270.	Gift Planning Officer	https://ift.tt/2rm5ywt

Latest Work at Home Jobs list

271. Entry Level Sales Representative (Minneapolis, MN)	https://ift.tt/35R0Oh
272. Start the New Year In Your Own Career! (Blaine)	https://ift.tt/2ZiC4Mr
273. Change Someone's Life/Work From Home-CCH (Hartford) (Hartford)	https://ift.tt/34OOtcf
274. Immediate Openings - Customer Sales/Service - Apply Now (Auburn)	https://ift.tt/34SA52y
275. Change Someone's Life/Work From Home-CCH (Putnam) (Putnam)	https://ift.tt/2PSsT2l
276. Entry Level Sales Representative (Western MD)	https://ift.tt/3979rGl
277. Change Someone's Life/Work From Home-CCH(Willimantic) (Willimantic)	https://ift.tt/2PU0p8x
278. Change Someone's Life/Work From Home-CCH (Bridgeport) (Bridgeport)	https://ift.tt/2EJkisv

Latest Work at Home Jobs list

279. Change Someone's Life/Work From Home-CCH (Danbury) (Danbury)	https://ift.tt/2MD0Odx
280. Change Someone's Life/Work From Home-CCH (Norwalk) (Norwalk)	https://ift.tt/2Qhfn7t
281. Lincoln, Benton, and Linn County- Part-time Foster Care?	https://ift.tt/2tGt9sw
282. Immediate Openings - Customer Sales/Service - Apply Now (Malta)	https://ift.tt/2PPc5cA
283. Immediate Remote Work - Customer Sales/Service - Paid Weekly (Junction City)	https://ift.tt/399jXwY
284. Youth Advocate - Residential Program [080] (Lake Oswego, OR)	https://ift.tt/2Zn0AMv
285. Senior Accountant - Part Time, Flex Hours (San Antonio Area)	https://ift.tt/34PpGEU
286. Business Loan Advisor- Position is base + bonus + commission (Remote) (Portland)	https://ift.tt/2rm3PqZ

Latest Work at Home Jobs list

287. Immediate Openings - Customer Sales/Service - Apply Now (Mentor, Chardon, Kirtland)	https://ift.tt/2Sl53xZ
288. Business Loan Advisor- Position is base + bonus + commission (Remote) (Boston)	https://ift.tt/2PSnwju
289. Life Insurance Sales (Boston, MA)	https://ift.tt/34QLa4v
290. Immediate Remote Work - Customer Sales/Service - Paid Weekly (Worthington)	https://ift.tt/2sZxtD6
291. Luxury Showroom Design Consultants Needed (Interior Design Background) (Atlanta)	https://ift.tt/35RyATF
292. Senior Accountant - Part Time, Flex Hours (Atlanta, GA)	https://ift.tt/34OONHZ
293. Life Insurance Sales (Springfield, MA)	https://ift.tt/39aC5XE
294. Senior Accountant - Part Time, Flex Hours (Harrisburg Area)	https://ift.tt/2QcnW3s
295. Immediate Openings -	https://ift.tt/2EP5O

Latest Work at Home Jobs list

	Customer Sales/Service - Apply Now (Hattiesburg, Oak Grove)	Y5
296.	Immediate Remote Work - Customer Sales/Service - Paid Weekly (Grand Forks)	https://ift.tt/35Q3Su5
297.	Senior Accountant - Part Time, Flex Hours (Twin Falls Area)	https://ift.tt/2sSDmBZ
298.	Senior Accountant - Part Time, Flex Hours (Reno)	https://ift.tt/374ymZO
299.	Part Time Openings - Paid Weekly - Interview Right Away (Florence, Muscle Shoals)	https://ift.tt/377CxUn
300.	Life Insurance Sales (Worcester, MA)	https://ift.tt/2s6l0NQ
301.	Senior Accountant - Part Time, Flex Hours (Charlottesville Area)	https://ift.tt/377CAQ3
302.	Immediate Remote Work - Customer Sales/Service - Paid Weekly (Baker City)	https://ift.tt/37dOQ1R
303.	Immediate Openings -	https://ift.tt/2PQ76

Latest Work at Home Jobs list

	Customer Sales/Service - Apply Now (Heath, Newark, Cambridge)	s9
304.	Immediate Openings - Customer Sales/Service - Apply Now (Stillwater, Blackwell, Cushing)	https://ift.tt/2QcQfyL
305.	Senior Accountant - Part Time, Flex Hours (Houston)	https://ift.tt/2QcQppR
306.	Inbound only (Customer Service) (Richmond)	https://ift.tt/399aCoT
307.	Luxury Showroom Design Consultants Needed (Interior Design Background) (Bellevue)	https://ift.tt/34OZLxk
308.	Part Time Openings - Paid Weekly - Interview Right Away (Lake Charles)	https://ift.tt/361MSkZ
309.	Immediate Openings - Customer Sales/Service - Apply Now	https://ift.tt/2t08dfD
310.	Bilingual Clinicial - ICC (all locations)	https://ift.tt/2PTJ7sd
311.	Clinician - ICC (all locations)	https://ift.tt/2rkWtUE

Latest Work at Home Jobs list

312.	Immediate Remote Work - Customer Sales/Service - Paid Weekly (Grand Island)	https://ift.tt/2rnPJ8H
313.	Account Manager (Birmingham, AL)	https://ift.tt/370DRsj
314.	Senior Accountant - Part Time, Flex Hours (Denver)	https://ift.tt/2sUmt9s
315.	FT Lead Kitchen & Reception Attendant (Lone Tree)	https://ift.tt/2QdrJ0h
316.	Tax Preparer - Pd Training starts Jan 9! (Multiple Locations)	https://ift.tt/2MlGaOG
317.	Immediate Remote Work - Customer Sales/Service - Paid Weekly (Scottsbluff)	https://ift.tt/35Mrvnr
318.	PT Front Desk Associate-Staybridge Suites-An IHG Hotel (Lone Tree-Park Meadows Mall Area)	https://ift.tt/2QcmcHf
319.	Luxury Showroom Design Consultants Needed (Interior Design Background) (Culver City, Santa	https://ift.tt/2MisfZR

Latest Work at Home Jobs list

Monica)	
320. Immediate Openings - Customer Sales/Service - Apply Now (Dunkirk, Fredonia)	https://ift.tt/373VBmw
321. Immediate Remote Work - Customer Sales/Service - Paid Weekly (Watford City)	https://ift.tt/2PPFZx8
322. Immediate Remote Work - Customer Sales/Service - Paid Weekly (North Platte)	https://ift.tt/370J9nC
323. Immediate Remote Work - Customer Sales/Service - Paid Weekly (Aberdeen, Bath)	https://ift.tt/34Tjrjo
324. Immediate Openings - Customer Sales/Service - Apply Now (Iowa City)	https://ift.tt/37dQNvd
325. Immediate Remote Work - Customer Sales/Service - Paid Weekly	https://ift.tt/2MmW2k4
326. Immediate Remote Work - Customer Sales/Service - Paid	https://ift.tt/37dQP6j

Latest Work at Home Jobs list

Weekly (Rapid City)	
327. Immediate Remote Work - Customer Sales/Service - Paid Weekly (Minot)	https://ift.tt/35R9eFB
328. Senior Accountant - Part Time, Flex Hours (Boulder Area)	https://ift.tt/375HaOK
329. Senior Accountant - Part Time, Flex Hours (Tallahassee)	https://ift.tt/2QcmTQR
330. Immediate Remote Work - Customer Sales/Service - Paid Weekly (Lincoln)	https://ift.tt/373Wpry
331. Systems Administrator at craigslist (financial district)	https://ift.tt/2KzF6r3
332. Security Analyst at craigslist (financial district)	https://ift.tt/2Zn1taA
333. Luxury Showroom Design Consultants Needed (Interior Design Background) (Upper West Side)	https://ift.tt/34RQTqG
334. Machine Learning Developer at craigslist (financial district)	https://ift.tt/30roC97

Latest Work at Home Jobs list

335.	Mobile App Developer at craigslist (financial district)	https://ift.tt/2I2tlb1
336.	React Developer at craigslist (financial district)	https://ift.tt/2HGeFLp
337.	Full Stack Web Developer at craigslist (financial district)	https://ift.tt/2I3s9nK
338.	JavaScript Developer at craigslist (financial district)	https://ift.tt/2HIOx2w
339.	Luxury Showroom Design Consultants Needed (Interior Design Background) (burlingame)	https://ift.tt/2tLxmLH
340.	Immediate Remote Work - Customer Sales/Service - Paid Weekly (Hermantown, Duluth)	https://ift.tt/2MD4ewT
341.	Immediate Remote Work - Customer Sales/Service - Paid Weekly (Ottumwa)	https://ift.tt/2Zhqkdj
342.	Immediate Remote Work - Customer Sales/Service - Paid Weekly (Sioux City)	https://ift.tt/2ZfqcuS
343.	Senior Accountant - Part	https://ift.tt/2Qhlp8

Latest Work at Home Jobs list

Time, Flex Hours (Portland)	d
344. Immediate Remote Work - Customer Sales/Service - Paid Weekly (Springfield, Chatham, Decatur)	https://ift.tt/2MnjIEW
345. DAY TRADE OUR MONEY - CORP. FUND MANAGER - NO INCOME CAP (Miami)	https://ift.tt/35UOzjO
346. Direct Support Professionals wanted!! (Santa Maria)	https://ift.tt/2Smaf4G
347. Immediate Openings - Customer Sales/Service - Apply Now (Bolivar, Richburg)	https://ift.tt/379u3MR
348. Immediate Remote Work - Customer Sales/Service - Paid Weekly (Cape Girardeau, Mount Vernon)	https://ift.tt/374pyTG
349. DAY TRADE OUR MONEY - CORP. FUND MANAGER - NO INCOME CAP (Twin Falls)	https://ift.tt/2QbqrTu
350. Sales/Mkting in health and	https://ift.tt/2ZfTc5

Latest Work at Home Jobs list

fitness	G
351. NO MORE 9-5 OR COMMUTE, MAKE AN EXECUTIVE LEVEL INCOME FROM HOME. (Des Moines)	https://ift.tt/34VOxXX
352. Luxury Showroom Design Consultants Needed (Interior Design Background) (Thousand Oaks)	https://ift.tt/2ELebUt
353. DAY TRADE OUR MONEY - CORP. FUND MANAGER - NO INCOME CAP (Houston)	https://ift.tt/2ELLc31
354. Immediate Remote Work - Customer Sales/Service - Paid Weekly (Decatur)	https://ift.tt/2QcUpXp
355. Immediate Remote Work - Customer Sales/Service - Paid Weekly (LaSalle, Peru, Yorkville)	https://ift.tt/2ELVwrx
356. Immediate Openings - Customer Sales/Service - Apply Now (Lafayette, Breaux Bridge, Carencro)	https://ift.tt/2EP7QY0
357. Immediate Remote Work -	https://ift.tt/2SrtQQ

Latest Work at Home Jobs list

Customer Sales/Service - Paid Weekly (Davenport, Clinton)	G
358. Immediate Remote Work - Customer Sales/Service - Paid Weekly (West Acres, Prairiewood)	https://ift.tt/2Zig0BL
359. Termite Scheduler (Glendale) (Glendale)	https://ift.tt/34P6VBD
360. Expanding God Based Green-Organics Technology Company (Summerville)	https://ift.tt/2QgJhlL
361. DAY TRADE OUR MONEY - CORP. FUND MANAGER - NO INCOME CAP (Virginia Beach)	https://ift.tt/39aH2Qe
362. Assisted Living - Med Aide - Senior Living Community (226) (Sherman Oaks)	https://ift.tt/2si9df8
363. Immediate Openings - Customer Sales/Service - Apply Now (Montgomery, Wetumpka)	https://ift.tt/376T3Eu
364. Group Home Staff + Hiring Bonus (Atascadero)	https://ift.tt/399hLFl

Latest Work at Home Jobs list

365.	Customer Service | Work from Home | Full-time | $10/HR| (All Nevada)	https://ift.tt/2QgJV99
366.	Immediate Remote Work - Customer Sales/Service - Paid Weekly (Sioux Falls, Harrisburg)	https://ift.tt/36Xn8Ge
367.	DELIVER PACKAGES — EARN UP TO $22/HR —	https://ift.tt/38ZZ3jU
368.	DAY TRADE OUR MONEY - CORP. FUND MANAGER - NO INCOME CAP (Colorado Springs)	https://ift.tt/2SlfcL6
369.	2020 Election Time At Luce Research	https://ift.tt/34NsrXd
370.	Customer Service | Work from Home | Full-time | $10/HR| (All Florida)	https://ift.tt/2SkgfuA
371.	Immediate Remote Work - Customer Sales/Service - Paid Weekly (Macomb, Colchester, Good Hope)	https://ift.tt/2PSuyoo
372.	Immediate Remote Work -	https://ift.tt/370Nve

Latest Work at Home Jobs list

	Customer Sales/Service - Paid Weekly (Reading)	s
373.	Customer Service Advocate (Lawrenceville, IL)	https://ift.tt/2rmVPpP
374.	Hiring All Positions (Burlington, MA)	https://ift.tt/2MoJ3hF
375.	Community Based Day Support Staff (Gardner and Orange MA)	https://ift.tt/2sVr4IT
376.	Immediate Remote Work - Customer Sales/Service - Paid Weekly (Egg Harbor Township, Absecon)	https://ift.tt/2t0fa0d
377.	Immediate Remote Work - Customer Sales/Service - Paid Weekly (Lancaster, Elizabethtown)	https://ift.tt/35S1hA2
378.	Hagar's House Advocate (Work-Housing Exchange) (Mid City)	https://ift.tt/2ZijfZX
379.	Hiring Kitchen Positions (Raleigh, NC)	https://ift.tt/2sTC0qu
380.	Hiring Restaurant Positions	https://ift.tt/2sSWx

Latest Work at Home Jobs list

(Phoenix, AZ)	vs
381. Direct Support Professional Staff (Paso Robles, CA)	https://ift.tt/37o32eD
382. Programming & Testing Positions	https://ift.tt/2sSXrlm
383. Metropolitan Property Group is looking for agents! Make 150k per year! (Flatiron)	https://ift.tt/35S0ijg
384. Hiring Restaurant Positions (Naples, FL)	https://ift.tt/35Xwhic
385. Personal Assistant to Super Cool High Profile Female Executive (San Francisco Bay Area)	https://ift.tt/34RTT6r
386. WORK FROM HOME or THE BEACH	https://ift.tt/2MlQhmC
387. Home Health Aide- Concepts of Independence (Bedford Hills NY)	https://ift.tt/34LEnsE
388. Office Assistant (Work From Home)	https://ift.tt/2EJrxR4
389. A Place At Home hiring now!	https://ift.tt/2sT0xvY

Latest Work at Home Jobs list

Employer of Choice 2019 (Littleton, Highlands Ranch, Parker, Castle Rock)	
390. Groundwork Coffee- Store Team Lead (Pico)	https://ift.tt/2rlJBO6
391. SOCIAL WORKER (San Luis Obispo)	https://ift.tt/2ENsHeA
392. QA Automation Engineer - Remote	https://ift.tt/2POkOf4
393. Marketing Assistant (santa rosa)	https://ift.tt/2rn1MTH
394. Make $200K+ in the 2020...Start Today. MAJOR OPPORTUNITY. (brooklyn)	https://ift.tt/2PPUnp7
395. Hiring Sous Chef NEW RESTAURANT OPENING (Silver Spring)	https://ift.tt/2MozkYP
396. Office Manager - Marketing (Tigard)	https://ift.tt/2Qkll7I
397. Online Retail / Rewards Program / Customer Service	https://ift.tt/2sXOIV0

Latest Work at Home Jobs list

	Representative (Omaha)	
398.	On call - Banquet Servers	https://ift.tt/2t1w9zh
399.	On Call - Bar Porters (Honolulu)	https://ift.tt/2Mppvdf
400.	Full Time Bookkeeper/Admin Posisiton - Remote	https://ift.tt/2ELpbkJ
401.	CNA and CHHA Students WANTED (Ridgewood NJ)	https://ift.tt/2EQMRUE
402.	Underground Construction District Manager needed (Cheyenne)	https://ift.tt/2ELtVXo
403.	Direct Support Professional Staff (San Luis Obispo)	https://ift.tt/2ro5i07
404.	ENTRY LEVEL MANAGEMENT POSITION (Ocala and more cities in ad)	https://ift.tt/2PRH3Rg
405.	Call Center Agent Second Shift (Woburn)	https://ift.tt/375WVVU
406.	Administrative Assistant / Office Manager (ARDEN)	https://ift.tt/2MlWbEi
407.	ART Restoration Tech	https://ift.tt/2sewE

Latest Work at Home Jobs list

	(Windsor NJ)	9i
408.	Easy $$$$ Help needed for overnight/weekend part pull assistance (Colonie, NY)	https://ift.tt/2EJBRZv
409.	Travel Agent Work From Home Position	https://ift.tt/35Tf2hF
410.	Appointment Setting/Work From Home (Denver)	https://ift.tt/2PPxRgk
411.	Part Time CPA (Wheat Ridge)	https://ift.tt/2sUHgKs
412.	APPOINTMENT SETTER/REHASHER NEEDED FOR HOME IMPROVEMENT COMPANY (MISSION HILLS)	https://ift.tt/2rlhpLe
413.	RN's & LPN's needed in Sun Prairie home (Sun Prairie)	https://ift.tt/2SmvC5Y
414.	Expanding Christian CBD-Organics Tech. Comp. Needs Serious Candidates (Sarasota)	https://ift.tt/2SglOdA
415.	Seasonal Recruiting Specialist (LOCAL CANDIDATES	https://ift.tt/2ZiKGCK

Latest Work at Home Jobs list

ONLY) (Palo Alto)	
416. Firecracker General Manager Trainee (Sterling, Virginia)	https://ift.tt/363zIDG
417. Business/Marketing Coach Needed $100K+ per year (Austin, but you work from your home)	https://ift.tt/34Ro65i
418. Call Center Agent (Woburn)	https://ift.tt/35TO89x
419. Appointment Setter (Woburn)	https://ift.tt/2sTbIoq
420. Leads Manager (The Colony, TX)	https://ift.tt/2ZhF3ow
421. Regional Property Manager Needed (Bellevue)	https://ift.tt/2ZoMla3
422. Customer Experience Specialist (Denver)	https://ift.tt/2SlbdOA
423. ACT/SAT Tutors--Training and Materials provided! $38-43/hr to start	https://ift.tt/2MDmXsb
424. Expanding Christian CBD-Organics Tech. Comp. Needs	https://ift.tt/34SHejq

Latest Work at Home Jobs list

	Serious Candidates	
425.	Auto Detailing Technician (Costa Mesa)	https://ift.tt/35TsiD3
426.	Operations Specialist (Downtown)	https://ift.tt/2SmIQ2k
427.	Data Entry (Downtown)	https://ift.tt/2sei7uh
428.	ACT/SAT Tutors wanted--flexible schedule--starting at $38-$43/hr DOE	https://ift.tt/372fV7W
429.	WANTED: SUPERSTAR BOOKKEEPER (San Marcos)	https://ift.tt/2PUbDdf
430.	WANTED: PERSUASIVE MEDICAL WRITERS, WORK FROM HOME (Los Angeles - Remote Work)	https://ift.tt/2s5QTWQ
431.	Cinematic Wedding Videographer Wanted for Consistent Work	https://ift.tt/2SrO2BY
432.	WANTED: PERSUASIVE MEDICAL WRITERS, WORK FROM HOME (Downtown)	https://ift.tt/2rj8f1M

Latest Work at Home Jobs list

433.	Custom Home Sales Consultant (Bend)	https://ift.tt/2ZhS41r
434.	Make a Difference in the Lives of Others (Tampa Bay)	https://ift.tt/2EPBLiZ
435.	Case Management Supervisor (santa rosa)	https://ift.tt/2Zj9c6L
436.	sign waver (ocean breeze)	https://ift.tt/393JlnT
437.	12 hr Day and Night Shift (Albuquerque)	https://ift.tt/2QkCQoq
438.	We are looking for people to book cruises and more from home. (Miami)	https://ift.tt/2SkuBez
439.	Full-time OVERNIGHT Guest Service Agent (Kaneohe)	https://ift.tt/2SnJP2b
440.	LEED/Energy Consulting - Project & BizDev Analyst (San Diego)	https://ift.tt/2Mpg8dn
441.	Case Management Specialist (4 day work week!) (Englewood)	https://ift.tt/2EToN3v
442.	Insurance Sales Agent	https://ift.tt/2Mnfg9

Latest Work at Home Jobs list

443. Appointment Setters Needed Now!! (Work From Home)	https://ift.tt/35RoPVL
444. Leasing Agent (Seasons Park) (Richfeild)	https://ift.tt/378aBjd
445. Bilingual (English/Spanish) Customer Care Specialist I (Portland)	https://ift.tt/395egjK
446. Field Technician with Extensive Telephony and Cabling Experience (Tulsa, OK)	https://ift.tt/393UgOu
447. Licensed Insurance Agent - Base + Uncapped Commission + Benefits	https://ift.tt/39h7Luq
448. Cultural Arts District Program Manager (Hillsboro)	https://ift.tt/35TmJEC
449. Join Our Team Today! --- DSP positions $16/hour (Portland)	https://ift.tt/2PQjkAO
450. PACE Facility-Administrative Support (Grants Pass)	https://ift.tt/2EKSUKA
451. SENIOR ACCOUNT	https://ift.tt/377QP

Latest Work at Home Jobs list

EXECUTIVE PUBLIC RELATIONS (Downtown Seattle)	VI
452. Account Supervisor - Public Relations (Seattle)	https://ift.tt/2ZhjhRI
453. Dietary Aide: Bellingham Healthcare (1200 Birchwood Ave.)	https://ift.tt/2ZgxDC0
454. Certified Nursing Assistant: Avamere Bellingham Healthcare (1200 Birchwood Ave.)	https://ift.tt/2ZnC6D4
455. Old School Newspaper Copy Editor Sought (Pasadena)	https://ift.tt/2tMb1h2
456. Are You A Data Entry Pro? Work From Home After A Year (Westlake Village)	https://ift.tt/2Zjmpwn
457. Transcriber (Work from Home)	https://ift.tt/2Qfxavz
458. WORK OVERNIGHT WITH NO EXPERIENCE! $5000 OPPORTUNITY AT HOME! (ANYWHERE)	https://ift.tt/2SnZ8rQ
459. HIRING Home Care Aides -	https://ift.tt/2PPYly

Latest Work at Home Jobs list

	Shoreline (Seattle)	g
460.	Home Care Aide - Ballard (Ballard)	https://ift.tt/2t0Z32s
461.	HIRING Home Care Aides to Work in University District (University District)	https://ift.tt/34Rw4M7
462.	Health Assistant II Mesa Vista (Oroville)	https://ift.tt/2PTaFO0
463.	Jamba Juice Team member (Redding)	https://ift.tt/2Zi3EcQ
464.	Immediate Openings @ Extra Hand In-Home Care,, (Ontario/Hesperia/Fontana/Rialto/Redlands)	https://ift.tt/2EOICzS
465.	Safety and Security Officer Metro Regional Center (https://ift.tt/1i8TCSb)	https://ift.tt/2Zl2iyc
466.	Groundwork Coffee- Barista Shift Lead (Rose)	https://ift.tt/2Ss1Lcl
467.	Outside Sales--appts set for you (Salem to Portland)	https://ift.tt/34PH2l5

Latest Work at Home Jobs list

468. Independent Travel Agent (San Diego)	https://ift.tt/2SIDLre
469. Work from Home (Florida)	https://ift.tt/2PSfOpl
470. Wellness Coach/Sales Associate (North Jersey)	https://ift.tt/2Mmszqm
471. New Office Mgmt Startup seeks Admin to share the load (Clark County & From Home)	https://ift.tt/2tEnaV5
472. Independent Travel Agent	https://ift.tt/2SIX5EP
473. Human Anatomy and Physiology Instructor Full-time Tenure-track Fall 2020	https://ift.tt/2QcITLz
474. Mathematics Instructor Full-time Tenure Track Fall 2020	https://ift.tt/2EZU5Gl
475. Medical Assisting Instructor Full-time Tenure-track Fall 2020	https://ift.tt/35RVN89
476. Biology Instructor Full-time Tenure-track Fall 2020	https://ift.tt/2PTT20S
477. $25.00 HR. (Work From	https://ift.tt/2PTipQ4

Latest Work at Home Jobs list

	Home) Secretary (West Des Moines)	
478.	Experienced Resume Writer (Bethesda)	https://ift.tt/39ab720
479.	Small Business Loan Affiliates Needed Potential $2-4K per week (Nationwide)	https://ift.tt/2SnExUu
480.	High 6 figure sales job (Remote)	https://ift.tt/2SmYc7c
481.	GROUP SALES JOB OPPORTUNITIES (Honolulu)	https://ift.tt/2s6saSf
482.	Tax Preparer- Training Starts Jan 9! (Pueblo)	https://ift.tt/34QN3xR
483.	TEAM RUN CLASS A OTR I5 RUN HOOK AND DROP (TRACY)	https://ift.tt/35Q5i88
484.	Work From Anywhere in the U.S. - Admin Account Manager (15-40 hrs/week (Folsom)	https://ift.tt/2seX7nb
485.	Appliance Repair Technician (Bozeman)	https://ift.tt/2tMIDvg
486.	K-12 Reading and Math	https://ift.tt/2sfE5wX

Latest Work at Home Jobs list

	Instructors (oakland piedmont / montclair)	
487.	Female required (Nottingham)	https://ift.tt/2sUlOUO
488.	Models Wanted	https://ift.tt/2Mnnw9I
489.	Work from Home - Dircct TV sales and more (your city)	https://ift.tt/2tKAfMF
490.	Administrative Assistant bilingual Eng-Spa (West LA)	https://ift.tt/2EKPx6g
491.	WORK FROM HOME: Hottest trend in the US ($3-5k p/t or $8-10k f/t)	https://ift.tt/2Q7YkVq
492.	Travel Agent - Work from Home	https://ift.tt/2EFpUns
493.	Make $1500 daily - Work From Your Home Office - FT/PT (San Antonio)	https://ift.tt/2SkOZMv
494.	Online Teaching (English)- $16-$22 hr (Atlanta)	https://ift.tt/2Q3PJ5O
495.	Make $1500 daily - Work	https://ift.tt/38Zzu2F

Latest Work at Home Jobs list

	From Your Home Office - FT/PT (Duluth)	
496.	Paralegal (Will also entertain admin. asst/other) (Mission Viejo)	https://ift.tt/36ZgiQz
497.	Online Teaching (English)- $16-$22 hr (Columbus)	https://ift.tt/397mCaO
498.	Online Teaching (English) - $16-$22 hr (Charlotte)	https://ift.tt/2MlYtDp
499.	Online Teaching (English)- $16-$22 hr (New York)	https://ift.tt/373pXpw
500.	HHA for Greater Pay!Without HHA? You can still get a GREAT PAY! (Midtown)	https://ift.tt/35IUQiB
501.	$5000-$10000+ A Month. Start Immediately! (Nationwide)	https://ift.tt/2MjGFc8
502.	ONLINE Coach: looking for flexibility/time freedom (Your laptop)	https://ift.tt/373ZYOH
503.	Online Coach- looking for flexibility and time freedom (Seattle (anywhere/home))	https://ift.tt/2sQUU1a

Latest Work at Home Jobs list

504.	Online Coach- looking for flexibility and time freedom (Work from Home/Laptop)	https://ift.tt/2EFOZi6
505.	Online Coach- looking for flexibility and time freedom (Laptop)	https://ift.tt/2tJq9vB
506.	Online Coach- looking for flexibility and time freedom (SLO/from home/anywhere you have Wifi)	https://ift.tt/2QbAGqT
507.	Online Fitness Opportunity {Not Personal Training} (Work From Home/Laptop/Anywhere)	https://ift.tt/2PKOLN4
508.	Cashier/Barista FT and PT (SEATAC)	https://ift.tt/2EL60aM
509.	Real Estate Sales Consultant (New York, NY)	https://ift.tt/2MkZ6NL
510.	AT HOME Telephone Secretary	https://ift.tt/2Mm6MPL
511.	$$$$$$$$$- MAKE OVER $1 MILLION IN A YEAR - $$$$$$$$$ (Texas)	https://ift.tt/2Zgzy9E

Latest Work at Home Jobs list

512.	Insurance Agent / CSR / work from home (Chicago)	https://ift.tt/2riQ509
513.	$$$$$$$$$- MAKE OVER $1 MILLION IN A YEAR - $$$$$$$$$ (North Carolina)	https://ift.tt/2QbM6e9
514.	$$$$$$$$$- MAKE OVER $1 MILLION IN A YEAR - $$$$$$$$$ (New York)	https://ift.tt/2PPfE2p
515.	CABLE/SATELLITE TECHS earn $1000/wk $500 Sign on Bonus FULL Training (Raleigh, Cary, Apex, Clayton,Garner,Zebulon)	https://ift.tt/2tK9MyX
516.	Outstanding PT Position for a Work-At-Home Professional (Southern NH)	https://ift.tt/2MfuXiL
517.	WORK FROM HOME: Hottest trend in the US ($3-5k p/t or $8-10k f/t) (Are you into Marketing?)	https://ift.tt/2MiLcLK
518.	Tutor Jobs Online! Explore Your Teaching Passion-From Home! (Princeton)	https://ift.tt/2EM5s4t

Latest Work at Home Jobs list

519.	Energy Rebate Specialists- $2,500 per Week (Chatsworth)	https://ift.tt/34QhGn4
520.	Direct Support Staff	https://ift.tt/34NPj9l
521.	Blackjack Pizza-Management-All Positions OPEN NOW(3 locations) (Denver-Aurora stores-START TODAY)	https://ift.tt/2MkRFGm
522.	Direct Support Staff (Denver)	https://ift.tt/2SeWkNH
523.	Ironworkers & Welders - Burlington, Western IL and Region	https://ift.tt/2MfHcMf
524.	Business Loan Brokers Wanted - NO LICENSE REQUIRED	https://ift.tt/36XTNLV
525.	MAKE UP TO $18/HR WITH POSTMATES! SIGN UP, EARN & CASH OUT SAME DAY!	https://ift.tt/2s0rxtn
526.	Personal Assistant Needed (Santa Fe)	https://ift.tt/2QhtwBl
527.	FEMALE Budtenders Wanted (Spring valley)	https://ift.tt/3732FQe
528.	NO MORE 9-5 OR	https://ift.tt/2Qc0B

Latest Work at Home Jobs list

	COMMUTE, MAKE AN EXECUTIVE LEVEL INCOME FROM HOME. (Chicago)	10
529.	Inbound Vacation Sales - Bilingual English/Spanish - Work From Home (Tampa)	https://ift.tt/2PNdDnh
530.	WORK FROM HOME: IMMEDIATE HIRE | NO FEES | FLEXIBLE HOURS ((Worldwide))	https://ift.tt/2ENKuIu
531.	WORK FROM HOME: IMMEDIATE HIRE | NO FEES | FLEXIBLE HOURS (Worldwide)	https://ift.tt/2sQ5qpA
532.	PT Customer Service Reps Needed!! (Midtown)	https://ift.tt/2Q8N0bz
533.	Savvy Marketers, Be Your Own Boss, Executive Income Potential	https://ift.tt/2Zhadwi
534.	Now Immediately Hiring Field Technicians Around ALABAMA (Pelham, Alabama)	https://ift.tt/2ZfHRCq
535.	Savvy Marketers, Work From	https://ift.tt/2SjA1X

Latest Work at Home Jobs list

	Home, Executive Income Potential	g
536.	Full-time On-Site Resident Apartment Manager ~ 54 units (santa clara)	https://ift.tt/2POBO4J
537.	Seeking RN, possibly LVN $37.50/hour (lafayette / orinda / moraga)	https://ift.tt/2EKHS8a
538.	Full-time On-Site Resident Apartment Manager ~ 77 units (sunnyvale)	https://ift.tt/2sPrErD
539.	Now Immediately Hiring Field Technicians Around MISSISSIPPI (Ridgeland, Mississippi)	https://ift.tt/2POx6UQ
540.	Sales Agent (Winter Haven, FL)	https://ift.tt/2Mkhmqs
541.	In Home Closer Needed! (Pittsburgh)	https://ift.tt/2ZeEawY
542.	In Home Closer Needed! (Greater Cleveland)	https://ift.tt/36WhO5S
543.	Contract Event Planner Part Time for NYC Firm (Midtown West)	https://ift.tt/393a8Rl

Latest Work at Home Jobs list

544.	costumer service Agent Work from home needed ASAP	https://ift.tt/2Q6EXMk
545.	INCREDIBLE WORK FROM HOME OPP! $2000-$5000 OVERNIGHT! START TODAY! (ANYWHERE)	https://ift.tt/2MhPp2o
546.	Grounds Supervisor/Specialist in Santa Rosa, CA (santa rosa)	https://ift.tt/2ZnuYXi
547.	***GAMECHANGER ~ Copy And Paste Your Way To 120K*** (Nationwide)	https://ift.tt/35ZhoMl
548.	FT/PT Work at Home No Experience Necessary	https://ift.tt/34KYyqM
549.	Assistant Office Manager (novato)	https://ift.tt/34TVjgQ
550.	Sales Representative (Danvers Massachusetts)	https://ift.tt/2riDjPe
551.	Sales Representatives Needed - Earn over $100k annually (Danvers Massachusetts)	https://ift.tt/2PLwYFo

Latest Work at Home Jobs list

552. Work at Home | INSIDE SALES	https://ift.tt/39710Ll
553. PT/FT Work From Home, Immediate Start-Up "No Experience Needed" (Omaha and surrounding area)	https://ift.tt/2Zf0R48
554. Foreign Currency Trader - Finance, Part Time, Work From Home (Gilbert/Scottsdale/Chandler/Peoria/Tempe/Remote)	https://ift.tt/2EWMcS1
555. Stock/Options Trader - Finance, Part Time, Work From Home (Littleton/Aurora/Boulder/Arvada/Fort Collins/Remote)	https://ift.tt/390M6GN
556. Foreign Currency Trader - Finance, Part Time, Work From Home (Littleton/Aurora/Boulder/Arvada/Fort Collins/Remote)	https://ift.tt/2PNqd5U

Latest Work at Home Jobs list

557. Foreign Currency Trader - Finance, Part Time, Work From Home (LA/Manhattan Beach/Santa Monica/Redondo Beach/Long Beach/Rem)	https://ift.tt/393sDFh
558. Stock/Options Trader - Finance, Part Time, Work From Home	https://ift.tt/2Q9NJsZ
559. Foreign Currency Trader - Finance, Part Time, Work From Home	https://ift.tt/2Mi7WM0
560. Foreign Currency Trader - Finance, Part Time, Work From Home (DC/Bethesda/Rockville/Alexandria/ Gaithersburg/Remote)	https://ift.tt/2MldLbr
561. *FT/PT Work at home, Start Today, NO Experience necessary (Anywhere)	https://ift.tt/372sxfq
562. Foreign Currency Trader - Finance, Part Time, Work From	https://ift.tt/34RZHwt

Latest Work at Home Jobs list

Home (Atlanta/Marietta/Alpharetta/Lawrenceville/Remote)	
563. Stock/Options Trader - Finance, Part Time, Work From Home (Newton/Framingham/Cambridge/Waltham/Remote)	https://ift.tt/35OT0Nd
564. Foreign Currency Trader - Finance, Part Time, Work From Home (Germantown/Franklin/Cordova/Murfreesboro/Remote)	https://ift.tt/394Qm7U
565. Stock/Options Trader - Finance, Part Time, Work From Home (Dallas/Flower Mound/Arlington/Garland/Remote)	https://ift.tt/2MlvPT8
566. Foreign Currency Trader - Finance, Part Time, Work From Home (Irvine/Huntington Beach/Anaheim/M. Viejo/Remote)	https://ift.tt/2MleIR3

Latest Work at Home Jobs list

567. rForeign Currency Trader - Finance, Part Time, Work From Home	https://ift.tt/34PzJKj
568. Foreign Currency Trader - Finance, Part Time, Work From Home (Dallas/Flower Mound/Arlington/Garland/Remote)	https://ift.tt/2EH1dXU
569. Foreign Currency Trader - Finance, Part Time, Work From Home (Orlando/Longwood/Boca Raton/Jupiter/Naples/Remote)	https://ift.tt/36Zvqxf
570. Stock/Options Trader - Finance, Part Time, Work From Home (Bellevue/Federal Way/Kirkland/Renton/Kent/Mt Vernon/Remote)	https://ift.tt/34PEbZr
571. H&R Block Receptionist (Tacoma)	https://ift.tt/2POcFqX
572. Foreign Currency Trader - Finance, Part Time, Work From Home	https://ift.tt/2SpiRXY

Latest Work at Home Jobs list

(Alexandria/Richmond/Chesapeake/Roanoake/Hampton/Remote)	
573. Foreign Currency Trader - Finance, Part Time, Work From Home (Bellevue/Federal Way/Kirkland/Renton/Kent/Mt Vernon/Remote)	https://ift.tt/35RCR9U
574. Stock/Options Trader - Finance, Part Time, Work From Home (Chicago/Naperville/Evanston/Arlington Heights/Remote)	https://ift.tt/2PNsTR0
575. Foreign Currency Trader - Finance, Part Time, Work From Home (Chicago/Naperville/Evanston/Arlington Heights/Remote)	https://ift.tt/34MDJuX
576. Foreign Currency Trader - Finance, Part Time, Work From Home (Annapolis/Bowie/Gaithersburg/Ellico	https://ift.tt/2Sj2891

Latest Work at Home Jobs list

tt City/Remote)	
577. Foreign Currency Trader - Finance, Part Time, Work From Home (Sandy/Layton/Orem/Lehi/Kaysville/Remote)	https://ift.tt/2ELOJ12
578. Stock/Options Trader - Finance, Part Time, Work From Home (Manhattan/Brooklyn/Hempstead/Staten Island/Jersey City/Remot)	https://ift.tt/36V95ku
579. Foreign Currency Trader - Finance, Part Time, Work From Home (Manhattan/Brooklyn/Hempstead/Staten Island/Jersey City/Remot)	https://ift.tt/2PRtEJb
580. Foreign Currency Trader - Finance, Part Time, Work From Home (Nashville/Chattanooga/Memphis/Murfreesboro/Remote)	https://ift.tt/36Yz4HR

Latest Work at Home Jobs list

581. Foreign Currency Trader - Finance, Part Time, Work From Home (St. Paul/Minnetonka/Eden Prairie/Osseo/Burnsville/Remote)	htttps://ift.tt/394NoAt
582. Foreign Currency Trader - Finance, Part Time, Work From Home (Philly/Cherry Hill/Bethlehem/Levittown/Remote)	htttps://ift.tt/2Q9jLoU
583. Foreign Currency Trader - Finance, Part Time, Work From Home (San Antonio/Austin/Round Rock/Katy/Sugar Land/Remote)	htttps://ift.tt/34HFgm4
584. Travel Agents Wanted (Santa Barbara)	htttps://ift.tt/2Sh8aH6
585. Foreign Currency Trader - Finance, Part Time, Work From Home (Sugar Land/Pasadena/Katy/Spring/The Woodlands/Remote)	htttps://ift.tt/2EJycuL
586. Foreign Currency Trader - Finance, Part Time, Work From	htttps://ift.tt/2MjGhu6

Latest Work at Home Jobs list

Home (Sacramento/Santa Rosa/Roseville/Chico/Remote)	
587. 100% Comp Loan Officers/Branch Managers up to $1,000,000 income (Santa Ana)	https://ift.tt/2ZmiD5x
588. Pharmacy prescription delivery RX (San Mateo)	https://ift.tt/2sempSf
589. PT/FT Work From Home, No Experience Needed! Immediate Start-Up! (Columbus and surrounding area)	https://ift.tt/2EQYye1
590. Registered Behavior Technician (RBT) in East Bay (berkeley)	https://ift.tt/2SeiQ9s
591. ... BECOME A Digital Marketing Consultant: Earn a Mil In 4 Years!... (Nationwide)	https://ift.tt/2MgzYHO
592. Travel Agents Wanted - Work From Home	https://ift.tt/2PKbuJ6
593. Work from Home Internet Analyst	https://ift.tt/2Zbo8E5

Latest Work at Home Jobs list

594. Behavior Interventionist - Entry Level Behavioral Health Position (Albuquerque, NM)	https://ift.tt/2txZSjE
595. Registered Behavior Technician (Deming, NM)	https://ift.tt/35Kdy9J
596. Behavior Interventionist - Entry Level Behavioral Health Position (Farmington, NM)	https://ift.tt/2Zd7yUm
597. Behavior Interventionist - Entry Level Behavioral Health Position (Shiprock, NM)	https://ift.tt/34PzIWQ
598. Part Time Customer Service Representative W Lebanon NH (Lebanon, NH)	https://ift.tt/35Jml65
599. Behavior Interventionist - Entry Level Behavioral Health Position (Roswell, NM)	https://ift.tt/2tHKwcJ
600. Registered Behavior Technician (Roswell, NM)	https://ift.tt/2SeVOPR
601. Registered Behavior Technician (Espaola, NM)	https://ift.tt/2MhuVXM

Latest Work at Home Jobs list

602.	Registered Behavior Technician (RBT) (Albuquerque, NM)	https://ift.tt/2sSYRCl
603.	Registered Behavior Technician (Bernalillo, NM)	https://ift.tt/2Q7lwD5
604.	Registered Behavior Technician (Hatch, NM)	https://ift.tt/2EIuscR
605.	Registered Behavior Technician (Santa Fe, NM)	https://ift.tt/2EH0xSi
606.	Spanish Speaking Registered Behavior Technician (Albuquerque, NM)	https://ift.tt/2Q7uEaN
607.	Behavior Interventionist - Entry Level Behavioral Health Position (Bloomfield, NM)	https://ift.tt/2SecOFN
608.	Registered Behavior Technician (Farmington, NM)	https://ift.tt/35M0Wij
609.	Native English Content Writer (£6/1000 words - view to increase) (Reading)	https://ift.tt/2Q8SMd5
610.	Behavior Interventionist - Entry Level Behavioral Health	https://ift.tt/2ZaXPOk

Latest Work at Home Jobs list

Position (Artesia, NM)	
611. ARTESIA - Behavior Interventionist Tuesday 3-6, Wednesday 3-5, (Artesia, NM)	https://ift.tt/38XsXVX
612. Remote (Work from home) Customer Service Position (30 openings) ((You (Your home)	https://ift.tt/35Gvylb
613. *Work From Home, Flexible Schedule, Executive Income Potential	https://ift.tt/35LaTwn
614. *Work From Home, High Earning Potential, Part Time	https://ift.tt/2scA5x4
615. Business secretary - PA, London (London)	https://ift.tt/2sP5LsA
616. Full Time - Crew 〇 - Service and Kitchen -〇 Full Time (Reno)	https://ift.tt/2rkHY3k
617. Trailer Loader / Washer W/ NEW PAY RATES & Advancement in Your Future (St.Paul, MN)	https://ift.tt/2SfARnV
618. ARE YOU MONEY MOTOVATED? EARN $1,000	https://ift.tt/2Q6rZhK

Latest Work at Home Jobs list

WKLY+COMM.!!!	
619. Weekend Courier Dispatcher Needed Sat-Sun Work From Home (Pinellas Park)	https://ift.tt/2sPd4Aw
620. DRIVE YOUR WAY Get your 2020 Started Right !!! (Metro Area)	https://ift.tt/2tyXbhM
621. Funding Specialist...Make $200K+ in the 2020...Start Today (brooklyn)	https://ift.tt/391EbbY
622. Telemarketing (no cold call no experience)work from home. $12hr&coms& (summerlin)	https://ift.tt/2s0gKPV
623. Skilled tradesman Position available (Madison and surrounding areas)	https://ift.tt/2sRXcNo
624. $5000-$10000+ A Month- Start Immediately! (Nationwide)	https://ift.tt/2Se0lwo
625. Online Teaching (English)- $16-$22 hr (Jacksonville)	https://ift.tt/2PKax3j
626. Remote Customer Service Representative (Norfolk, VA)	https://ift.tt/2Q83fFB

Latest Work at Home Jobs list

627. Certified Travel Agent - home based (Cincinnati)	htttps://ift.tt/36XWkph
628. Telemarketing (no cold calls/no exp. necc)work from home. $12hr&coms& (naples)	https://ift.tt/34Qe6cV
629. sign waver (Hobe Sound)	https://ift.tt/2ZcZgfo
630. Work From Home-Sale Consultants Needed-Start Immediately (Louisville and Surrounding Areas)	https://ift.tt/2EFJdwZ
631. Are you a great communicator - Join our Team!!!! (davie)	https://ift.tt/2ZcLWaF
632. Work From Home-Independent Reps-Start Immediately (Seattle and Surrounding Areas)	https://ift.tt/2PLwOOA
633. All-around Home, Kitchen and Bath Remodeler (san jose downtown)	https://ift.tt/2ZbFbWs
634. Operations / Marketing Assistant - Remote/Work from home	https://ift.tt/2tGQ0Eu

Latest Work at Home Jobs list

635.	Are you thinking of giving up your health and life insurance license? (PRESCOTT VALLEY)	https://ift.tt/2QaXO8W
636.	On-Site Apartment Manager ~ Campbell ~ Part-time (campbell)	https://ift.tt/36XIYtd
637.	On-Site Apartment Manager ~ Mountain View ~ Part-time (mountain view)	https://ift.tt/2PM3lnn
638.	*** Work From Home -Phone Sales Master - Timeshare Exit Strategies *** (Home Office)	https://ift.tt/2Zf6e36
639.	*** Work From Home -Phone Sales Closer - Timeshare Exit Strategies *** (Home Office)	https://ift.tt/38V6FnM
640.	$1000.00/Day Returning Phone Calls (Hartford)	https://ift.tt/2SmyAXM
641.	$1000.00/Day Returning Phone Calls (Anchorage)	https://ift.tt/2Mkn5MZ
642.	Make $17/hr plus tips assembling furniture!	https://ift.tt/35M0Cjx
643.	$1000.00/Day Returning	https://ift.tt/2Q9Uiv

Latest Work at Home Jobs list

	Phone Calls (Seattle)	G
644.	Administrative Assistant (LaGuardia - Astoria/East Elmhurst Queens)	https://ift.tt/2ETRDRH
645.	WORK FROM HOME-6 FIGURE INCOME POTENTIAL (Phenix City)	https://ift.tt/36XRuIH
646.	Rapid Tax Class to Start This Week! (FORT WALTON BEACH)	https://ift.tt/2ZfftjO
647.	TRAVEL AGENT--Work from Home-Commission Based (Nationwide)	https://ift.tt/36VSAVo
648.	HIGH-END LISTING BROKER / Seeks MktPtnr/Protege and Weekend Warriors (Allstate California)	https://ift.tt/2scnERX
649.	Sell From Home! (Homebuyer Grants USA Nationwide)	https://ift.tt/2ZcgbOY
650.	Community Manager (Tucson)	https://ift.tt/2SeicZp
651.	Make $17/hr assembling	https://ift.tt/393Xb

Latest Work at Home Jobs list

	furniture before Christmas!	Xm
652.	Retail Fashion Store Manager (Downtown)	https://ift.tt/2Sfulbd
653.	Work From Home -Surveys (Remotely)	https://ift.tt/2Zb2sbh
654.	Medicare Billing Specialist (ft meyers)	https://ift.tt/2Zcwag1
655.	"$10K- $20K A Month - Start Today"' (Statewide)	https://ift.tt/2sVry1u
656.	Furniture Assemblers Wanted! $20/hr (plus tips)	https://ift.tt/2Zg6hM5
657.	STYLIST (Uptown- 17th and Downing)	https://ift.tt/36Zr8Ga
658.	Model Maker to build Architectural and Museum scale models (Seattle)	https://ift.tt/370nz2F
659.	Used Car salesman "Work from Home". (Temecula)	https://ift.tt/2Sg39hX
660.	RETURNING PHONE CALLS & GETTING PAID FOR IT (St.	https://ift.tt/2MjmKKy

Latest Work at Home Jobs list

Augustine)	
661. RETURNING PHONE CALLS & GETTING PAID (Tampa)	https://ift.tt/34KtuYe
662. Estheticians and aspiring estheticians needed. $600-$1200 per week (Lakeview)	https://ift.tt/2MkbMEk
663. Not the average Personal Support Worker (Gold Beach/Brookings)	https://ift.tt/2SeFZIH
664. Tudor Jobs Online! Explore Your Teaching Passion-From Home! (Princeton)	https://ift.tt/2PJOxFY
665. Social Media & Marketing Intern	https://ift.tt/36UMIvq
666. WILDLIFE CONTROL CAREER: NO EXP. NECESSARY w/ GREAT BENEFITS! (SCHAUMBURG)	https://ift.tt/34R7r1X
667. FOREST RANGER-LIKE CAREER w/ WILDLIFE CONTROL Firm: NO EXP. NECESSARY	https://ift.tt/2sdc9d7

Latest Work at Home Jobs list

(SCHAUMBURG)	
668. Travel Agent | Gateway Travel (Work From Home, Part or Full Time)	https://ift.tt/2ZnMl4H
669. Creative Manager (B2B SaaS Audio/Video Podcast Producer/Photographer) (Denver, CO (RiNo))	https://ift.tt/2sZOBbu
670. Inbound Business Development Representative (BDR) (Denver, CO (RiNo))	https://ift.tt/2SkZejO
671. Insurance Customer Service Representative | $17 per hour (work from home)	https://ift.tt/2Q8GzVS
672. Residential Property Manager (Des Moines)	https://ift.tt/2SjLypp
673. Material Handler (Colonial Heights)	https://ift.tt/398kbEE
674. Want a REWARDING Career? Full Time and Part time work! Apply Today	https://ift.tt/2QcdAAp

Latest Work at Home Jobs list

675. Warehouse Supervisor $34,805 M-F, Day Shift + Benefits (Fort Myers)	https://ift.tt/3993Mjd
676. Warehouse Asst. Branch Manager-M-F/Day Shift/Up to $45k first year (Ft. Myers)	https://ift.tt/2Zh9mfO
677. Digital Nomads needed- Teaching job (Remote)	https://ift.tt/2QckrKm
678. DSHS DDA Case Resource Manager Non-Permanent (Thurston County - Tumwater)	https://ift.tt/2Sk635i
679. Resident Assistant (Full Time- Part Time) Mornings & Overnights (Brooklyn Park, Brooklyn Center and New Hope)	https://ift.tt/2QgTIBw
680. Online Retail / Rewards Program / Customer Service Representative (Richmond)	https://ift.tt/34PrpKo
681. Mail and Package Delivery Associate (redwood city)	https://ift.tt/2SkRm20
682. Work from home - Major E-	https://ift.tt/374LCg

Latest Work at Home Jobs list

Commerce Company	Y
683. Auto Body Parts Coordinator Entry Level (berkeley)	https://ift.tt/377Olkn
684. Registered Nurse/RN: Avamere Bellingham Healthcare (1200 Birchwood Ave.)	https://ift.tt/2Mp2Ttk
685. Warehouse Associate (Stocker) - $16.50 (Hayward) (hayward / castro valley)	https://ift.tt/2EPxZWU
686. Service Desk Associate - $17.00 (Hayward) (hayward / castro valley)	https://ift.tt/371mLdO
687. Tool Rental Sales Associate - $16.50 (Santa Clara) (santa clara)	https://ift.tt/35RHb99
688. Start your Real Estate Career Century 21 Trains New Agents (Northland & Overland Park & Blue Springs)	https://ift.tt/2MqBFT3
689. Gentlemens Club Waitresses, Dancers, Hostesses (Houston)	https://ift.tt/2rlavpt
690. Accounting Technician-Inspire	https://ift.tt/2SkNZ

Latest Work at Home Jobs list

	School of Arts and Sciences (Chico, CA)	YO
691.	Administrative Specialist- Inspire School of Arts and Sciences (Chico, CA)	https://ift.tt/2Mkt5VW
692.	MISSION BBQ COME JOIN THE TEAM (MIDLOTHIAN HULL ST)	https://ift.tt/2PNcYSJ
693.	Social Media & Marketing Manager	https://ift.tt/398G0US
694.	*Be Your Own Boss, Flexible Schedule, Work From Home	https://ift.tt/2SlNIVH
695.	WILDLIFE CONTROL CAREER: NO EXP. NECESSARY w/ GREAT BENEFITS! (SCHAUMBURG and CHICAGO)	https://ift.tt/36WopgM

Latest Work at Home Jobs list

Remotees - Jobs List

Title	Links
• Scrapinghub: Senior Backend Engineer	https://ift.tt/2rljOFT
• Kinsta: WordPress Support Engineer - Asia Pacific	https://ift.tt/34PK4Wz
• Clevertech: Java/Spring Developer [REMOTE]	https://ift.tt/373NwOU
• Clevertech: Ruby on Rails Engineer [100% REMOTE]	https://ift.tt/398MdzO
• Clevertech: Tech Lead [100% REMOTE]	https://ift.tt/2SiBhK8
• Clevertech: Senior React Developer [100% REMOTE]	https://ift.tt/34RZyJs
• Clevertech: Sr. Backend Engineer- Node.JS [100%	https://ift.tt/392jTzn

Latest Work at Home Jobs list

REMOTE]	
• Clevertech: Sr. Full Stack Developer, Node/React [100% REMOTE]	https://ift.tt/34PaJTh
• Clevertech: Software Quality Engineer [100% REMOTE]	https://ift.tt/2s4Xi4B
• FineTune Learning: QA Engineer (gherkin, selenium, requirements analysis, QA metrics)	https://ift.tt/2EKjuDt
• GrammaTech: Senior Software Engineer/Architect (Remote in USA may be possible)	https://ift.tt/2POO1qi
• Comcate: Customer Success Manager	https://ift.tt/2ELgxm6
• TaxJar: Engineering Manager	https://ift.tt/397r7C4
• TaxJar: Full-Stack Software Engineer	https://ift.tt/2Znru6X
• TaxJar: Salesforce	https://ift.tt/2Q9oaIw

Latest Work at Home Jobs list

Administrator	
• IDx Technologies: Senior Dev Ops Engineer	https://ift.tt/3967rON
• TaxJar: Partner Marketing Manager (Service / Tax Advisors)	https://ift.tt/2SnDfZI
• TaxJar: Partner Marketing Manager (Technology-Partner Program)	https://ift.tt/2Qr9zbJ
• TaxJar: Data Product Manager	https://ift.tt/34LPnWY
• TaxJar: Growth Product Manager	https://ift.tt/2QiPcx0
• Prism: Staff Reporter, Criminal Justice (remote)	https://ift.tt/2EP6j4e
• GrammaTech: Senior Software Engineer Architect	https://ift.tt/397tFjs
• Modern Tribe: Agency Marketing Content Specialist	https://ift.tt/2MpRyJp
• Source Coders: Senior Big	https://ift.tt/374G8Tc

Latest Work at Home Jobs list

	Data Software Engineer (Scala, Python or Java) - Onsite(SF) or Remote	
	• CrossBraining: Lead Front-end developer	https://ift.tt/2SkPMgr
	• Optimiso Group SA: Software Engineer, Full Stack (C# / Angular) - remote	https://ift.tt/2QdGiAO
	• Neybox Digital: Senior iOS Developer	https://ift.tt/2sSmhll
	• CrossBraining: Lead Front end Developer	https://ift.tt/2Mkr2kJ
	• Sun Life: Senior Software Engineer Back End	https://ift.tt/2EMdieu
	• The New York Times: Backend Software Engineer	https://ift.tt/390hmpn
	• Eco: Back End Engineer	https://ift.tt/2ZeKXqx
	• GitLab: Backend Engineer Verify	https://ift.tt/2tJcp41
	• General Awnings: Account	https://ift.tt/2sSSu23

Latest Work at Home Jobs list

Specialist	
• Teramind: Pre-sales Engineer	https://ift.tt/2ZnF0Ys
• flanksource: Kubernetes Site Reliability Engineer	https://ift.tt/2SfyUaZ
• Theorem: Experienced Backend Engineer - Go	https://ift.tt/2sOvAsE
• Theorem: Experienced Backend Engineer - Ruby	https://ift.tt/35MB7P9
• Aptera Software: Mobile Developer (Remote or Onsite)	https://ift.tt/395FqqW
• Enova: Senior Software Engineer	https://ift.tt/36ZPlwk
• Echo Bravo: Junior/Mid full-stack Developer	https://ift.tt/2SguBfG
• Secureworks: Software Engineer Platform Engineering	https://ift.tt/36Y1gKT
• New Context Services: Senior Go Developer	https://ift.tt/2sbWvhZ

Remote OK - Jobs List

Title	Links
o Senior Software Engineer Architect	https://ift.tt/2EPCyQM
o Senior Software Engineer Back End	https://ift.tt/35Upzti
o Backend Software Engineer	https://ift.tt/2rl0RmL
o Back End Engineer	https://ift.tt/2ShV7oN
o Backend Engineer Verify	https://ift.tt/2ZfIEU0
o Pre-sales Engineer	https://ift.tt/2PNgNay
o Kubernetes Site Reliability Engineer	https://ift.tt/2MlaSr7
o Senior Software Engineer	https://ift.tt/36VNLeK
o Software Engineer Platform Engineering	https://ift.tt/2rg0EB6
o Senior Go Developer	https://ift.tt/2sUOs9C

We Work Remotely

Title	Links
➢ TaskDrive: Sales Representative (x2)	https://ift.tt/2MELXiL
➢ LoyalTek: Customer service during evenings and/or weekends (Work at home)	https://ift.tt/2ENe4b1
➢ Caroline LaBass Health Care: Virtual Assistant	https://ift.tt/394dB2b
➢ Echo Bravo : Junior/Mid full-stack Developer	https://ift.tt/2Q5pHPM

That's All Friends. Let's meet again in my next edition

Latest Work at Home Jobs list

Want to see a daily list of Work From Home JOBS?

> Join this brand-new community in Reddit.
>
> Encourage discussion on jobs posted within 24 hrs.
>
> Join now!!!
>
> # r/Onlinejobs24 hrs

For advertisements contact me above. Kindly follow the below link to place your blog ad -
https://forms.gle/USBvCPsb1nzaxMoQ9

Latest Work at Home Jobs list

Latest Work at Home Jobs list

Disclaimer

The view points in this book are those of Rajesh Kunnatheeri. These views are based on his personal experience in the online Jobs. The intention of this book is to help Work at home and remote work aspirants to find genuine jobs. All the links given in this ebook are taken from the internet, and no effort is made to verify the genuineness of those links. Your use of the Service is at your sole risk. The Service is provided on an "AS IS" and "AS AVAILABLE" basis. The Service is provided without warranties of any kind, whether express or implied, including, but not limited to, implied warranties of merchantability, fitness for a particular purpose, non-infringement or course of performance.

Latest Work at Home Jobs list

ABOUT THE AUTHOR

The author, Rajesh Kunnatheeri, has been into online and offline jobs for the past 15 years. He got extensive experience in his chosen field and now started sharing his knowledge through ebooks, articles, YouTube videos. He is passionate about connecting jobs seekers with opportunity online. In his own words, "success with online jobs, lies in the ideas. If you can think and come up with a novel idea, then you are bound to be successful, of course, the idea should have a greater appeal."

www.ingramcontent.com/pod-product-compliance
Lightning Source LLC
Chambersburg PA
CBHW060842220526
45466CB00003B/1213